MARGINALIZATION OF GORKHAS IN INDIA

A COMMUNITY IN QUEST OF INDIAN IDENTITY

K.R. SHARMA

T.C. DAS

ABHIJEET PUBLICATIONS

DELHI 110094

ABHIJEET PUBLICATIONS
2/46 Tukhmeerpur Extension
Delhi-110 094
Phone: 011-22960492, 65698474
E-mail: abhijeetpublication@gmail.com

MARGINALIZATION OF GORKHAS IN INDIA: A COMMUNITY IN QUEST OF INDIAN IDENTITY

Second Edition 2025
First Published 2011

ISBN 978-93-81136-11=9

Rs. 780/-

PRINTED IN INDIA

Published by J.K. Singh for Abhijeet Publications, Delhi-110 094, Lasertypeset by Gaurav Graphics, New Delhi and Printed at Himanshu Printers, Delhi.

Preface

Writing the present book entitled "MARGINALIZATION OF GORKHAS IN INDIA—A Community in Quest of Indian Identity", we the authors, had to keep the objectivity that had interwoven with the Gorkhas of their living in the country over the period of last five hundred years or so both in the Indian Himalayas and mainland of the country. At every turn of their life, they had been marginalized by the mainstream communities instead of their dedication to the nation building process of the country. The present study is mainly based on the experiences of the authors in North-East India including the Darjeeling hills. In fact, the Gorkhas are concentrated in Darjeeling-Sikkim Himalayas. About one crore Gorkha population are living in India today without any specific identity realization by the mainstream communities of the country. The Gorkhas are serving the nation in militia, agrarian belts, plantation frontiers and service sectors of the country in the process of nation building endeavours. The present study shall highlight as to how the Gorkhas instead of having their contribution to the nation building endeavours are hardly recognized and brought under the mainstream of national life. The study universe is Darjeeling, Dooars and Terai areas of West Bengal in particular and North-East India in general. In the process of marginalization of Gorkhas in India, an analysis has been made both from the micro level and macro level taking into account of the genuinenss of the problems of the Gorkha community in India. How intra-community marginalization as well as inter-community marginalization processes are on vogue in the Gorkha community of the country is another objective of the study. How holistically, the Gorkhas are marginalized in the democratic country like India today is still another objective of the study. The study has also incorporated a case study of Gorkha tea plantation workers of Darjeeling to establish the fact that how the Gorkhas as a whole have been marginalized in the country. Marginalization is the social process of human society in which a major group marginalizes the other minor groups. For instance, in West Bengal, the Bengalis have marginalized the Gorkhas ever since the independence of the country. This marginalization process called for the emergence of a new theory palatable to a marginalized community like Gorkhas as the existing theory which binds the community like Bengali in West Bengal can not explain the real problems of the Gorkha community of Darjeeling-Dooars areas of West Bengal as well as North East India. So, the present study tries to evolve a new theory of social dynamics of the Gorkhas in India in general and at West Bengal in particular.

Working on the research project, we were fully supported by our wives and children and we are

MARGINALIZATION OF GORKHAS IN INDIA
A COMMUNITY IN QUEST OF INDIAN IDENTITY

Contents

1

Introduction

The Gorkhas are known to the world as vigilant soldiers with all sorts of sincerity, stubbornness and kindheartedness across the world (Northey and Morris: 1976). Coming to the question of their immigration across the Himalayas, it is found that they made the entire Himalayas as their abode putting all their sweats, blood and lives. Their aspiration for national identity has to be however recognized with the history of five hundred long years of their living in India. The Indians know that they are very sincere soldiers having superb martial characters. But their martial endeavours have gone into dust bin as their struggle for acquiring Indian identity has so far been hardly taken into due consideration by the Indians. Simply they are known for manual workers, chowkidars, soldiers and bodyguards of big sorts or aristocrat families of the Indian metropolis.

The present work is the outcome of thirty informal years of research study of the authors regarding the marginalized status of Gorkhas and Gorkha tea plantation workers of North-East India. The marginalized status of the Gorkha tea plantation workers is prototype of the entire Gorkha community of North-East India at the micro level research analysis. Being the Gorkhas by ethnicity, we, Dr. K.R. Sharma and Shri T.C. Das have perceived the same glimpses of life while interacting with the central communities of the country. Simply, the so-called big sorts among the Gorkhas are made Shields (*Moharas*) of the other communities of the country. It means that the Gorkhas are marginalized from both within the respective community and from other mainstream communities of the country. In the present study, we have tried our level best to analyze the process of internal and external marginalization of the Gorkha community with our personal life experiences as well as the case study of tea plantation industry of North- East India including Darjeeling hills.

The Gorkhas and Gorkha tea plantation workers are mainly concentrated in tea plantations and agrarian belts of Darjeeling-Dooars areas of West Bengal and the state of Sikkim of North-East India. Their immigration history from Western Himalayas is the history that started in 15th century. The original Gorkhas from India immigrated to Western Nepal, Gharwal, Sikkim, Darjeeling and North-Eastern Himalayas including Assam to save their Gow Dharma (cow-Hindu religion) from the treacherous attacks of Muslim rulers including their Indian followers. The push factor for their immigration to Indian Himalayas from the Nepal Himalayas was poverty, caste rigidities and aspiration for class enrichment. That had lead to the emergence of male immigration to Indian mainland (*Munglan*—the land of Mogals) in search of jobs particularly in Indian armies and other forces. It is found that the Gorkhas also joined the army of

Kauravas during the great Mahabharata war. In fact, then, there was no specific political boundary between present India and Nepal. The same was the picture in respect of other countries adjoining India like Burma, Bhutan and Sikkim as well as Manipur, Nagaland, Mizoram, Tripura, Assam, Meghalaya and Arunachal Pradesh of North East India. This was the main reason as to why the people used to move freely from one corner of Indian sub-continent to another.

Even the present country like Bengladesh had no specific political boundary with India which helped Bengalis of Bengladesh to move freely to the present West Bengal state and settle down permanently. Similar was the case of Gorkhas of Nepal who being acclimatized in the Himalayas preferred to settle in the Himalayan regions of East and North-Eastern India including Maynmar. The same thing is also found in case of North-East India where people from Burma, Thailand, Tibet etc. migrated and settled down in various regions of North-East India (Bose:1997) permanently. Still today, we found that some people of North-East India visit their relatives' homes very frequently especially at the time of festivals and ritual ceremonies. In quest of survival, some communities among others tried to make better living than other communities by following the process of marginalization. So, marginalization is the alpha and omega of human civilization. The process of marginalization has lead to the emergence of inter-ethnic rifts and struggle for better existence. The specific characteristic features of these highlander communities are shaped by the isolated Himalayan jester, culture and languages/dialects which are mostly dissimilar to Indian mainland communities.

The above observation indicates that the Gorkhas along with other ethnic communities of North-East India were the boarders of the same boat in the pages of history in so far as their immigration history in the region is concerned. The pertinent point is that some communities immigrated little bit earlier in the region than the other communities. In fact, since the time when those communities had been immigrated from Burma, Thailand, Tibet etc. to North-East India, also the Gorkhas (Kshatriya and Brahmins) of India were immigrating to Nepal Himalayas. This may be the obvious reason why the present Indian Gorkhas immigrated to Indian mainland a little bit later than they immigrated to the Himalayas. From this perspective, if we can analyze the history of whole communities of the region, we find that every ethnic community had been the immigrated community to the region. So, it is really misnomer to call only the Gorkhas as immigrants from Nepal. In fact, the Gorkhas were the immigrants from India to Nepal once upon a time during the Muslim rule in India.

Gorkha Immigration to North-East India

Talking about Gorkha immigration to the Eastern Himalayas consisting of Darjeeling, Sikkim and Bhutan, it is found that it was 1652 A.D. when Chowgel dynastry started at Sikkim, few Newars (goldsmiths) were invited to Sikkim to mint coins (*Chaptay Paisa*). This along with the introduction of settled cultivation (terrace cultivation), a large number of Gorkhas especially, Bahun, Chhetri, Mangar, Gurung, Kami, Damai, Sarki, Rai, Limbu, Thami, Tamang,Gurung etc. were invited to Sikkim-Darjeeling by the then Chowgel kings of Sikkim-Darjeeling. It was because of this fact that to have sustainable revenue source, settled cultivation was a Must for the Chowgel kings. The local Sikkimese Lepchas and Bhutias were not accustomed to have such terrace cultivation of sustainable nature. It shows by the revenue history of Nepal (Regmi: 1971) and Western Indian Himalayas that only the Gorkhas were the exponents of terrace cultivation in the Himalayas (Sharma; 2005). This is even found today at Arunachal Pradesh (Sharma: 2003) where the local tribes have leased out their land for terrace cultivation to the Gorkhas no matter whether they are from Nepal, Assam or other places of North-East India. The history of Gorkha immigration to the then undivided Assam is found to be the history of five hundred long years when Ahom kings used to rule the present entire Assam consisting of present entire North-East India. The terrace cultivation along with *Gai Goth* (cow sheds) as well as animal husbandry of the Gorkhas attracted the Ahom kings as it used to provide good revenue to the government of Ahom kings. This was the main reason why the Gorkhas did not like to join tea plantation jobs later on in Assam when the British planters started tea cultivation in Assam. By the time, tea cultivations had started in Assam, the Gorkhas were already well received and recognized by the local government for settled cultivation in the region. Later on, the same strategy was followed well by the other government of North-Eastern states in so far as the question of settlement of the Gorkhas in North East India was concerned. This fact has been well found to be exposed when we visited Manipur, Nagaland, Arunachal Pradesh, Meghalaya, Tripura, Mizoram and Assam during 2002-2006 A.D. Here, in this respect, whosoever the Gorkhas are there, they are mainly concentrated in rural areas of the region. Miles together, we found the *Gai Goths* (cow sheds) of the Gorkhas. Almost all the lands having terraces in hill areas are raised by the Gorkhas for settled cultivation. So, they have made the land cultivable making fertile with cow dung and other natural fertilizers. In this way, the settled cultivation of the respective state governments of North East India, gave rise to end to some extent the Jhum cultivation of the local tribes. This is the main reason why the terrorist outfits of local tribes today of North East India do not like to have more and more Gorkhas in the region being supported by their governments for state revenue. Of course, this is the main reason why the Gorkhas are being evicted through the whole hearted socio-economic, cultural as well as political marginalization processes of the mainstream communities of the region. The state governments are also the covert supporters of the process of marginalization of Gorkhas by the mainstream communities and terrorist outfits as no concrete action is being taken by the governments of North- East India against such terrorist outfits whenever the Gorkhas are ousted or ejected from the region by such terrorist outfits.

Pondering on the immigration history of Gorkhas in Eastern Himalayas particularly the Bhutan and Sikkim along with Darjeeling, it is found that the Gorkhas are again concentrated in the rural niches of the region. It is also found that at first Gorkhas were not preferred for tea garden jobs because the Adivasis as tea garden workers were recruited in Darjeeling hills between 1840 to 1848-49 from Santhal Parganas, Ranchi and other places of Bihar, present Chattisgargh and Orissa, but those Adivasis could not however work in the hill tea gardens as they could not adjust with the adverse climate of hills and therefore they were replaced by the Gorkhas from various parts of Darjeeling hills and also a few couples from the Nepal Himalaya's in and around 1850 A.D. Interestingly, there is no accurate account of labour immigration at the tea plantations of Darjeeling hills from Nepal. Thus, it is all about the utter speculations or presumptions that all the tea plantation workers of Darjeeling hills are hailed from Nepal.

It is really a politically motivated Bengali chauvinist politics to call Gorkha tea plantation workers of Darjeeling hills as the immigrants from Nepal. In fact, the then Nepalese Government of Nepal was antithetical to supply tea garden workers at Darjeeling from Nepal. This was the main reason why the British planters recruited the Gorkha Sardars and Gallawalas (labour recruiters) to recruit their respective caste/tribal workers from their places of origin. Here, the places of origin as mentioned by some scholars are very vague as not a single specific account has been found to have stated so far regarding the accurate places of origin of the recruited workers of hill tea gardens. Of course, culturally, linguistically, emotionally and racially, all the Gorkhas draw their traditions from the mainland of Nepal.

In the research analysis, it is found that not a single worker could utter the actual place of origin of his/her ancestors. In fact, we had a haunch to explore the rationality behind blemishness of calling Gorkha tea plantation workers as immigrants in the region and found instead of their settlement history of more than two hundred years at the plantation industry, they are whimsically called immigrants and descendents of immigrants from Nepal. But finally, after intensive investigation, we found that they are all baseless blemishes as not a single tea garden worker wants to leave tea garden and go to Nepal for their settlement permanently. Some people go to Nepal just to meet their relatives there in the same manner as some Bengalis of West Bengal/North-East India go to Bengaladesh particularly Shylet district of Bengladesh for the such purpose. If it is so, can we call all Bengalis and North East India including West Bengal as the Bengaladeshi immigrants to West Bengal of North East India?— certainly not and the same is to be established in case of the Gorkhas of West Bengal and North-East India as all the Gorkhas have settled here permanently giving their blood, sweats and perseverance to the land of their settlement. The same thing is also found in case of Bhutan and Sikkim where the Gorkhas actually made the land cultivable, habitable and worthy to lead comfortable life for all the communities of these countries. But Gorkhas today are simply being used as "USE AND THROW COMMODITY" (*Kam Chalo Bharo Afal Tero Tharo*)—and this prevalent process we have operationalized in the study as the Marginalization process of entire Gorkhas and at the plantation society we have conceptualized the marginalization process of the Gorkha tea plantation workers of Darjeeling Himalayas in terms of the Plantation Sociology—the effort of specific theory building in the period of globalization of 21st century. It is the need of the hour to explore a suitable theory for the Gorkha community and Gorkha tea plantation workers in so far as the sociological theory building is concerned in the globalized era.

Why the Gorkha Migration Taken Place?

Culturally, the Gorkhas, since time immemorial, had deep conviction for male mobility across the countries and connect the workplaces with their home. It is said in Nepali proverb that *"CHORA KO JAT KI RAN MA KI BAN MA"* which indicates the fact that the son of a Gorkha family should either die in War field or in Jungle, to survive either by defeating the wild animals or enemies or die while fighting with the wild animals or enemies. It clearly shows that the Gorkha community was in the habit of globalizing their community people since time immemorial in the Himalayas. So, globalizing the Gorkha community as a whole, they had to encounter with the process of marginalization everywhere. Therefore, the globalization and marginalization are two sides of the same coin for the Gorkha community. But instead of the marginalization of the Gorkha community, it survives due to having their perseverance, stubbornness, sincerity, commitment, discipline and dedicated services to the global communities and thus they belong to Khati Kahnee Jati (Sharma:2005) or labourous community in the world. This is the main reason why the world knows that the Gorkhas as the martial race and therefore famous in war front but hardly the Gorkhas are known as the integral part of the working class of the world. The present study highlights the facts that they are equally a committed workforce of the industrialization as well as urbanisation processes. The example is the present study that highlights about the tea plantation industry of India particularly of North-East India where they are serving with all commitment and dedication for centuries together but marginalized by the national mainstreams. Thus, marginalization is the characteristic feature of the Gorkha society as a whole and the tea plantation workers of Gorkha community in particular.

Of course, the globalization as antithetical ethos in the past to the Indian working class has appeared to have been the positive impacts among the Gorkhas and Gorkha tea plantation workers as it has helped to liberalize the Gorkha community of India from the centurion old segregation, subordination and thereby marginalization. At least now, the Gorkhas and Gorkha tea plantation workers can not be made serfs or slaves at the plantation frontiers and North-East India. The present study highlights on the one had the impacts of globalization of Gorkhas on Gorkha tea plantation workers and marginalization of the Gorkhas and Gorkha tea plantation workers on the other. Both the processes are overwhelming forces to generate a new type of theory building in studying such a kind ethnic group of working class having most marginalized status in the country. The theory has been generated from the study which is called Theory of Plantation Sociology or the Sociology of Ethnic Marginalisation which is quite dissimilar to the centuries old Theory known as Industrial Sociology ever evolved during the British rule in India and neo-colonial post independent rule of Sovereign, Democratic and Republic India through the Government of West Bengal.

Defining Plantation Sociology is a herculean and de-novo task. It starts with the very nomenclature of plantation because the plantation is neither purely agriculture nor absolutely industrial unit of production. It is an agriculturally dominated industrial unit. It can neither be labelled as industrial organization in very true sense of the term nor can it be called as an agricultural unit having agrarian characteristics. Thus, the Plantation Sociology is the Sociology of industrial organization guided by the Sociology of agrarian social structure because apparently the Sociology of the industry is as good as the Sociology of rural hamlets that are found around the plantations. So, the Plantation Sociology is the synthesis of Industrial Sociology and Rural Sociology. It has distinctively a peculiar form of social system that is neither prevalent in an ideal industrial organization nor in a typical agrarian niche of the country. The mode of production is industrial but relation of production is purely agrarian regulated by Minimum wages being articulated by the industrial level tripartite agreements, minimum fringe benefits and most marginalized status of the workers among the industrial labours of the country. All the plantation workers are being defined alike under the Plantation Labour Act, 1951 coupled with the system of recruitment on *Badli* (substitute) basis. The workers recruited under the *Badli* system of labour recruitment can be ousted from the employment like the agricultural workers of the big Zamindars in Indian villages because the tea plantation workers have not been supposed to serve with the termination of service notice as per the provisions of the Industrial Disputes Act, 1947. Thus, the relation of production between the labours and management is as good as the agrarian production relation. In this way, the plantation workers are marginalized today in the period of globalization in so far as the provisions of Plantation Labour Act, 1951 are concerned.

The study is centered round the North-East India. In North-East India, the Gorkhas and Gorkha tea plantation workers are mainly concentrated in

Darjeeling-Dooars of West Bengal and Sikkim states. However, Sikkim being a separate state, the extent of marginalization from above i.e., the government level is at the lowest ebb but the marginalization of the Gorkhas and Gorkha tea plantation workers is at the highest level in West Bengal as West Bengal government belong to the Bengali community—the most *Subidabadi* (opportunist) community of the country. The West Bengal Government is merely concerned with the revenue from tea plantations, tourism industry, agrarian belts and urban areas for socio-economic development of Bengalis of West Bengal as it has nothing to do with the socio-economic development of the Gorkha community of Darjeeling-Dooars region of West Bengal.

At the tea gardens as well as other areas of Darjeeling-Dooars, the remote control mechanism lies with the Bengalis in so far as the *modus operandi* of the tea plantations and other economic sectors of the region are concerned. A few local vendors of the plantations and agrarian sector as well as urban sectors of West Bengal in the form of trade union leaders, management personnel cum owners as well as government officials helped to extend and establish the marginalization process of the Gorkhas and Gorkha workers in all aspects of their life. Talk about the trade union leaders, they are Bengalis, talk about the management, they are all belong to Bengali community and again talk about the West Bengal Government officials, they are all the Bengalis of West Bengal. So, a triangular matrix of management, trade union and government is responsible factor for the formation of marginalization of Gorkhas and Gorkha tea plantation workers of West Bengal. Unlike Adivasi workers who have their Jharkhand state, the Gorkhas and Gorkha tea plantation workers of the region do not have any specific state to represent them in India or abroad. This is another reason for evolving a new theory of Sociology known as Plantation Sociology or Sociology of Ethnicity to study the Gorkhas and Gorkha tea plantation workers in India including West Bengal. The proper assessment of human resource capital of the plantation industry and agrarian sectors with urban sector economy under the globalization process has been kept aside by the process of marginalization as West Bengal Government has adequate nostalgia for socio-economic development of the Gorkha community including the Gorkha tea plantation workers. Of course, with all political motives rarely, the government tries to launch some stray programmes for the Gorkhas and Gorkha workers keeping in view of merely the upliftment of the Gorkhas and Gorkha workers rather than the overall socio-economic development of the community and the workers as a whole.

The appropriate theory for this upliftment paradigm of Gorkhas and Gorkha tea plantation workers is the theory of Plantation Sociology or Sociology of Ethnicity. Secondly, the new theory is meant for the upliftment of Gorkhas and Gorkha tea plantation workers rather than development especially ever since the independence of the country in 1947. The theory is based on communal Bengali ethnic orientations especially launched by the West Bengal Leftist Government for the last 33 years as Leftists believe on caste/community politics based on ethnic nationalism (ethnocentric-chauvinism) rather than the class politics (Ganguli:2010) for the working class of the country.

The marginalization of Darjeeling-Dooars is apparent from the Siliguri-centric as well as Kolkata-centric (Debnath: 2009) development process of Bengalis and Bengal Government. The statement can well be supplemented by the fact that the Bengalis are concentrated at the towns where all the infrastructural, financial and holistic development funds are under the process of diffusion. Inspite of having Darjeeling town as district headquarters ever since the British days, the development strategy is at the lowest ebb compared to the Siliguri town over the last two decades. Citing unstable political situation in Darjeeling hills as a cheap slogan by the Siliguri Bengalis led by Shri Asok Bhattacharjee, the Municipal and Urban Development Minister, the Government of West Bengal has been spending all the funds at Siliguri and thereby marginalizing the Darjeeling hills. This is the government way of marginalizing the Darjeeling hills. Secondly, historically the Darjeeling-Terai-Dooars had never been with West Bengal or at the hand of Bengalis of West Bengal. Here, in this context, Prof. Anand Gopal Ghosh (2010), the prominent historian of North Bengal University, has once stated that historically, the entire Darjeeling-Sikkim Himalayas as well as sub-Himalayan Terai/Dooars and parts of Coochbehar had been inhabited by Kiratas—Rai, Limbu, Tamang, Gurung, Mangar, Lepcha, and Rajbanshi—the Koch people. Interestingly, he has not mentioned anything about the Bengalis in these areas and thus it appears from his observation that entire present Bengalis of the region are immigrants from the then East Pakistan and present Bengladesh. According to Prof. B.K. Mishra of North Bengal University, prior to the merger of North Bengal to the British Raj, there was no Bengali in North Bengal except a few Bengali Sanyasis (Sadhus) from South Bengal and the Bengali Sanyasis had no *locus standi* in North Bengal. The factor of Bengali immigration from Bengladesh to Himalayan and Sub-Himalayan belts made themselves conscious so as to marginalize the local innocent tribal Kiratas who mainly belong to Gorkha community and Rajbanshis. This is how the eternal marginalization process is working well for the Gorkha community.

At the micro level analysis, we would also like to cite an instance as to how the marginalization of Gorkha community takes place among the Gorkhas only. Here is a case study of Dr. K.R. Sharma who was marginalized as a Gorkha personality under the process of marginalization in the region, that too at the highest academic level. Dr. K. R. Sharma, a young man from the Gorkha community of 22 years hailing from Kalimpong of Darjeeling district at North Bengal University in 1981 completed his M.A. in Sociology and Social Anthropology. In fact, he was highly impressed by his post graduate mini thesis writing project that was conducted at Purbong Busty of Kalimpong where all the people belonged to the Gorkha community. Their pitiable socio-economic conditions invited him an urge of pursuing himself for research study. But for the next two years after 1981, he had to loiter here and there at Kathmandu, Sikkim and Kalimpong in search of a suitable job but alas in vain. Finally, at the end of 1984, Dr. Tanka Bahadur Subba, a research scholar from Kalimpong, inspired and encouraged him to leave teaching job that Dr. Sharma was doing at the Government High School, Kalimpong and join the research project being launched at the University of North Bengal for hill Darjeeling. So, he had to join the University of North Bengal as a Research Assistant at the Centre for Himalayan Studies. The name of project was Eco-Development Project—a project of Ministry of Environment and Forest, Government of India. Here, at that juncture, he was given impression by Dr. T.B. Subba and his teacher, Prof. N.C. Choudhury that along with his working in the project, he could do his Ph.D. and both of them also ensured him to provide a job when opportunity comes at the university. Working in the project for the next three years, he tried his level best to get his Ph.D. synopsis registered but Prof. Choudhury, somehow played dirty Bengali politics and did not encouraged him to do the same. Finally, in 1986, Dr. T.B. Subba, the then lecturer at Centre for Himalayan Studies of North Bengal University, somehow under his guidance got Dr. Sharma's Ph. D. synopsis registered. This was the way how for almost three years, he as a Gorkha research student was marginalized by his own teacher on the one hand and by his own community person on the other. But by the time Dr. Sharma's synopsis was registered, Dr. Sharma was on his crucial stage of life in so far as his age limit to get a government job was concerned.

In the meantime, Shri Kamal Kumar Sharma, the friend of Dr. T. B. Subba informed and suggested Dr. Sharma to apply for the post of Education Officer at the Central Board for Workers Education under the Ministry of Labour, Government of India. So, Dr. Sharma did the same considering his age to get the government job and the crisis of getting a suitable job. Fortunately, Dr. Sharma was selected from the Nepali speaking group but he had to leave the research project at the University of North Bengal and joined as Education Officer Trainee at the Indian Institute of Workers Education, Bombay. That ends Dr. Sharma's NBU chapter. But Dr. Sharma sensed the politics of ethnic marginalization accurately at NBU during 1986 when he applied for the post of Research Assistant at the Department of Sociology and Social Anthropology, University of North Bengal, Darjeeling. Here too, his project supervisor (Prof. N.C. Choudhury) was the Chairman of the interview committee. As per the impression given by Prof. Choudhury, he was damn sure that he would be getting the job, but Prof. Choudhury being a Bengali selected a Bengali friend of Dr. Sharma, Shri Prasanjit Deb Barman for the post. That made Dr. K.R. Sharma really frustrated but later on he came to know that his project supervisor (Prof. N.C. Choudhury) and Research supervisor (Dr. T. B. Subba) had concertedly decided not to give the post of Research Assistant to Dr. K.R. Sharma.

Later on, after joining the job of CBWE as Education Officer at Siliguri in 1987, Dr. K.R. Sharma tried to continue his research work under Dr. T. B. Subba, but he straightway rejected to do so due to the instigation of Dr. Subba's friend, Shri Kamal Kumar Sharma who was also then an Education Officer in Central Board for Workers Education at Siliguri. Dr. Subba rejected to guide Dr. K.R. Sharma for research work objecting on Dr. Sharma's personal matter and the matter was his marriage with Sarita Chhetri, M.A. B. Ed. So, Dr. K.R. Sharma had to leave the idea of doing his research under Dr. T.B. Subba. But after some time, Dr. Mita Bhadra, the wife Dr. Sharma's teacher, Prof. R.K. Bhadra, asked Dr. Sharma to talk about the research work with Prof. R. K. Bhadra of the department of Sociology and Social Anthropology, University of North Bengal.

Dr. Sharma did the same and started a fresh research work on Cinchona Plantation Workers of Darjeeling hills. So, under Prof. R.K. Bhadra, Dr. Sharma did his Ph. D. in 1996 and thus he became a doctorate for the first time in his life.

Here in this context, Dr. Sharma was marginalized both at the micro as well as macro levels. At the micro level, Dr. T. B. Subba hailing from the same ethnic community marginalized Dr. Sharma may be due to his fear psychosis that academically Dr. Sharma would be at par with him in so far as the academic pursuit is concerned. Still later on, Dr. Sharma came to know that the friend of Dr. Subba named Shri Kamal Kumar Sharma had misguided Dr. T.B. Subba against Dr. Sharma not to guide him for his Ph.D. thesis. The case study shows that Dr. Sharma's micro level marginalization from his own community fellows. Talking about the macro level marginalization, Prof. N.C. Choudhury being a Bengali thought it better to provide the job of Research Assistant to another Bengali who once happened to be the batchmate of Dr. Sharma. After acquiring his Ph.D. degree, Dr. Sharma approached Prof. R.K. Bhadra, his guide for a job at the University of North Bengal. But he too asked Dr. Sharma to try in hill colleges of Darjeeling because he also might have felt that Dr. Sharma too would be again at par with his Bengalis at NBU. Dr. Sharma found the NBU to be the colony of so-called Bengali academicians mainly hailing from Kolkata. Again, Dr. Sharma approached Prof. R.K. Bhadra to help him to get registered for his post doctoral synopsis. Dr. Bhadra again suggested Dr. Sharma to write more and more books rather than pursuing on post doctoral research study. However, for the last 25 years, Dr. Sharma has been pursuing himself on academic writing and published nine to ten books so far on Gorkha cinchona and tea plantation workers of North-East India and very shortly Dr. Sharma is going to get his post doctoral degree.

Analyzing Dr. Sharma's marginalization episode, two things have been explored and the exploration leads us to draw a tentative generalization that Gorkha society is infected by all sorts of individualism in so far as its social upliftment as well as development is concerned.

A. Marginalization leads Dr. Sharma to face challenges both at the micro as well as macro levels, and,

B. Make a place for Dr. Sharma in the academic world.

At the micro level, after pursuing research on cinchona plantation workers, Dr. Sharma was obstructed as well as intterrupted thoroughly on the office works by Shri Kamal Kumar Sharma, his own fellow Education Officer from his own community. This again had further negatively positivised Dr. Sharma's heart to do some concrete academic works by way of completing his Ph.D. Thesis. Here, the role of his beloved wife, Smt. Sarita Sharma is always commendable and appreciable. It is because of her active association and supports, Dr. Sharma did his Ph.D. At the macro level again, the same Dr. Mita Bhadra tried to exploit Dr. Sharma in many ways as Dr. Sharma was by ethnicity a Gorkha but somehow Dr. Sharma managed Dr. Mita Bhadra who used to sabotage Dr. Sharma by instigating her husband, Prof. R.K. Bhadra (Dr. Sharma's guide) to delay in going through Dr. Sharma's Ph.D. manuscript. So, Dr. Sharma being a Gorkha was positively inspired to face challenges with all stubbornness both at the micro as well as macro levels. In fact, Dr. Sharma promised himself to do something different so as to bind Dr. Mita Bhadra and Kamal Kumar Sharma to call him Dr. K.R. Sharma in course of time to come on and he did it and now both of them have to address him as Dr. K.R. Sharma as his name is there in the department as one of best Education Officers of CBWE from North East India and at the national level website. In fact, at the micro level, Dr. Sharma was awarded by the Central Board for Workers Education, Ministry of Labour and Employment, Government of India as the best Education Officer from North-East India in 2009 with the name Dr. K.R. Sharma only. Mr. Kamal Kumar Sharma, now Regional Director, CBWE, Siliguri chapter has to address him as Dr. K.R. Sharma. So, at the micro level also, Dr. Sharma's marginalization helped him in turn to go constantly ahead with his academic and professional pursuits. This might be the apparent reason why by the end of 2010, Dr. Sharma has planned to definitely complete his post doctoral research. Putting Dr. Sharma on the marginalization track by the people so described above inturn helped Dr. Sharma to himself gallop ahead to the process of his mainstreaming to the highest academic world and this is the living example of Gorkha sentiment, glory and stubbornness as a whole.

Dr. Sharma's sense of challenging the marginalization process is a prototype of entire Gorkha community. The challenges that Dr. Sharma took up will definitely be a glaring example that should encourage the future Gorkha scholars to comfortably go ahead in contributing and enriching the literature on marginalized Gorkhas and Gorkha tea plantation workers of our country in general and North East India in particular.

Operationalization of the Concept of Study

The process of marginalization of Gorkhas and Gorkha tea plantation workers is an unheard phenomenon as nobody knows anything in details about the Gorkhas and Gorkha tea plantation workers. In general, the Gorkhas are known as martial race suitable to the militia job that carries sincerity, commitment, stubbornness and loyalty to the masters and commanders. Their contribution to the Indian economy by working at tea plantation frontiers of North-East India has been for the first time introduced by the present scholars. Their utter marginality has been realized today in the period of globalization as Darjeeling hill Gorkhas and Darjeeling tea industry (universe of the Study) falls under the fair trade certificate along with other international certificates provided by the international customers especially U.S.A.. Interestingly, the fair trade policy has been administered for the tea products and not for the Gorkha workers who produce the fair trade orthodox tea for the international buyers. The marginalization is the characteristic feature of Gorkha community and therefore the Gorkha tea plantation workers. In order to operationalize the marginalization concept, following observation on Darjeeling tea plantation workers has been made with our experience of last thirty years of research study in Darjeeling. The marginalization process has been operationalized giving a theory and the theory is the Theory of Plantation Sociology or

Sociology of Ethnicity. The marginalization of an ethnic community by another community takes place after the span of long history of living together in the same geographical niche.

History of Marginalization of the Gorkha Tea Plantation Workers

The history of Gorkha tea plantation workers of Darjeeling Himalayas coincides with the history of marginalization of Gorkha ethnic community of the region. In the present section, we have tried our label best to historically describe the ways and means of marginalization of Gorkha tea plantation workers in Darjeeling hills. The marginalization of Gorkha tea plantation workers is the history of marginalization of Gorkha community in North-East India. Besides Gorkhas, there are Adivasi tea plantation workers in West Bengal but the Adivasi tea garden workers of Dooars/Terai and Assam have national existence as they have Jharkhand, Orissa and Chattisgargh states in India while the Gorkha tea plantation workers along with the whole Gorkha community as a separate ethnic community do not have any state of their own in India and therefore they have been still considered as immigrants or descendents of immigrants from Nepal by the mainstream communities of the country inspite of having five hundred years of their settlement in various parts of Darjeeling hills and North-East India (Sharma: 2010).

The marginalization history of Gorkha tea plantation workers can be classified into three phases, viz., British era, post-independent era and globalized era. In the study, the marginalization of Gorkha tea plantation workers has been found to be a holistic process of organized exploitation as the workers have been marginalized by all stakeholders of tea industry and society as a whole. The tea plantation workers are considered as peripheral entity while tea economy is central to all concerned whenever Indians including the Bengalis talk about the economy of Darjeeling hills.

Historically, ever since its inception from 1840, the marginalization of Gorkha tea garden workers of Darjeeling hills started with the recruitment of workers by the respective Gorkha caste and tribal Sardars and Gallawalas. In the process, first of all, the respective caste/tribal Sardars followed the method of luring their respective caste and tribal people to join the tea garden jobs stating that *"CHIYA KO BOT MA PAISA FALCHA"* meaning thereby the tea bushes provide ample as well as easy money to the workers. Here, the process of marginalization was telling lies to the people concerned and cheating them later on at the plantation enclaves. It shows that the push factor for labour migration from agrarian belts of Eastern Himalayas to the tea estates of Darjeeling hills was the caste and tribal sentiments and emotions that were being well played by the respective Sardars and Gallawalas (Sharma:1997). Interestingly, it is found that there is no specific account of labour migration from Nepal as blemished by the present West Bengal Bengalis because the recruitment of workers then was to be kept at the top secret by the management of tea plantations. Secondly, during the formative period of tea industry at Darjeeling hills when there was labour shortage, the then Nepal Government banned her citizens from joining the tea garden jobs at Darjeeling or *Munglan* (India—land of Muslims) except to be the *Lahurees* (soldiers in British

Gorkha Regiment at Lahore—now Pakistan). The term *Lahuree* emerged as they had to go to Lahore—the then headquarters of British Gorkha regiment. This may be the apparent reason why Prof. Sukomol Sen (1977) has stated that Darjeeling tea garden labours had been hailed from the local areas only. Geographically, then the entire eastern belts of Nepal adjoining Darjeeling hills were under inaccessible dense forests. So, there was no question of importing tea garden labours from Nepal. Of course, a few workers had joined Darjeeling tea garden manual jobs after the opening of Terai belts of Nepal (1950) with the eradication of malaria programme by the United Nations Organization (UNO).

The indentured nature of recruitment at their places of origin was supplemented by the forceful marriages on the ways before arriving at the tea gardens of the region. Doing this, the married couples could not run away with the hazardous nature of jobs at the plantations as well as unhealthy enclaves of the tea plantations. Therefore, living at isolated tea garden enclaves made them marginalized not only from the mainstream life but also the management and supervisory categories of the plantations.

Living at the respective caste and tribal labour *Dhuras* (labour lines) made each caste and tribal Gorkha tea garden workers marginalized from other castes and tribes having divergent dialects. Thus, socio-culturally, every caste and tribal Gorkha labour was marginalized from other castes and tribes. That was a kind of planters/managers'articulated marginalization process. Every worker had to seek permission from the planters/managers while pursuing any kind of socio-cultural activities in the garden including the marriage of their children. Many beautiful daughters of the workers had been made the victims of carnal sexual desires of the British tea planters. This may be the concrete reason why many Anglo-Indian families are still found at the tea gardens of Darjeeling hills today. Politically, the workers were encouraged to struggle for separate territorial jurisdiction for Darjeeling hills from the mainstream of West Bengal (Nag: 2008). It was a kind of British political gimmick on the ground that if the British Government was really interested for separate political existence of Darjeeling then how for the eleven hours on 15th August, 1947, the East Pakistani flag (Pradhan: 1978) had been hoisted at the top of Capital Cinema Hall of Darjeeling town? In this way, the Gorkha tea garden workers in particular and Gorkhas in general were to be fully marginalized. Here the parameter of marginalization was telling lies by the British planters so that they could easily manage their tea gardens without any disturbance from the local people and then the so-called Communists of West Bengal. The spectacular feature of the process of British marginalization of Gorkhas and Gorkha tea garden workers was of the overt type i.e., established exploitation which was the apparent means for marginalization because the tea gardens along with the entire Darjeeling hills were enclaves, isolated, indentured and low wages and employment of husband, wife and children (Bhowmik: 1981) units of British economy. It however became a covert type after the independence of the country.

During the British period, each caste and tribal Gorkha worker had to work under the respective Sardars. So, Sardari system was the prevalent method of labour recruitment, employment and administration of workers at Darjeeling hill tea gardens. The Sardars used to get Rs. 10/- as recruitment Bonus at the time of Dashara (Dasai) and the Sardars therefore used to act like employers, guides, guardians as well as the benefactors of the workers. Under the marginalization process, the workers had to compulsorily visit Sardars' hearth and homes at the time of Dasai to receive Tika (cultural blessings). In this way, they used to converge into a marginalized hieararchy (class) and thus they were made peripherals in the local social system. The colonial planters with colonial government became hundred percent successful to marginalize the Gorkhas and Gorkha tea garden workers in respect of socio-economic as well as political aspects of their life in the region. Politically, each tea garden had its own democracy which was called **Plantocracy** (Devi: 1989). In fact, democracy in India is the political system for the majority community, by the majority community and of the majority community (Subba: 1990). The Gorkha tea garden workers had been marginalized both at the micro level as well as at macro level. At the macro level, the Gorkha workers along with the entire Gorkha community had been marginalized in the region with the ethnic identity crisis and at the micro level, the colonial exploitation in the tea garden enclaves. The marginalization in the literature indicates as the process of making a minor group or community marginalized by the major group. The Gorkha tea garden workers of Darjeeling hills were made marginalized under the white colored British colonialists during the British period as ruling class and after the independence of the country under the ruling neo-colonial Indian owners, government mechanisms and planters-management. The common feature of marginalization of Gorkhas and Gorkha tea garden workers after the independence of country is the continuation of colonial legacy of dividing the Gorkhas and Gorkha tea garden working class into groups, factions, socio-cultural groups as well as religious sects by the West Bengal Government with the politics of Bengali Sakuni/Chanakya Niti.

Literature Survey

There is hardly any study on the marginalization of Gorkhas and Gorkha tea garden workers in India. The study of Prof. Sharit Bhowmik (1981) on Class Formation in the Plantation System depicts how the Adivasi tea garden workers of Dooars region of West Bengal had been fallen into the category of working class in spite of having distinct socio-cultural living of their own. The study by Virginius Xaxa (1997) indicates the existence of dual characters of tea plantation industry in the Dooars region of West Bengal. The Women Workers of Tea Plantations in India (1992) by Dr. Mita Bhadra shows as to how the women tea plantation workers have to adjust themselves as housewives and workers with the problems of their dual roles in tea industry in India. There are many other empirical studies conducted in various parts of the country on tea plantation workers and the Gorkha community in India but none of them are centered around the ethnicity aspects of workers on the one hand and none of the studies tried to explore as to how the Gorkhas and Gorkha tea plantation workers are really marginalized with reference to North-East India. Hence, the present study tries to explore the ways and means of Marginalization of Gorkhas and Gorkha Tea Plantation Workers in India. Doing this, the present study tries to evolve a new theory and the theory has been coined as the **Theory of Plantation Sociology or Theory of Ethnicity**. The study is also based on our earlier research study done and published with the title known as **Globalization and Plantation Workers in North-East India** (2009).

Methodology of the Study

In the study, the Social-Economic Anthropological approach has been adopted by visiting Gorkha workers households and other Gorkhas of North-East region of India with compact structured questionnaire. The study has also been done on the basis of participant observation method of Anthropology. The Gorkha tea plantation workers of Darjeeling hills along with other Gorkhas of the North Eastern region of India were closely observed. The rationale behind the selection of Darjeeling-Dooars tea industry and Darjeeling hills is due to the single most reason that Gorkha tea plantation workers and Gorkhas in majority are found in only Darjeeling-Dooars areas of West Bengal. About thirty thousand Gorkha tea plantation workers are there in Dooars-Terai areas of West Bengal. About one crore Gorkhas are living today in the country. There is hardly any significant percentage of Gorkha tea plantation workers in Assam as well as other North Eastern Indian tea plantations. Whatever the Gorkhas are there in Assam and other north eastern region, they are mainly concentrated in agrarian niches of these states of North-East India. The Darjeeling-Dooars tea industry and Gorkha tea plantation workers are two sides of the same coin. Almost 52,000 Gorkha tea plantation workers are there in Darjeeling hills. The anthropological observation of marginalization process of Gorkhas and Gorkha tea plantation workers of Darjeeling hills and

Dooars forms an interesting research proposal for intensive investigation. The method appears to be the most suitable ones to the scholars like us as we belong to the same community ie. Gorkha Community and Gorkha tea garden workers mainly belong to Darjeeling-Dooars. Initially, we were not wholly accredited as well as recognized by the Gorkhas and Gorkha tea garden workers for our research study but after six months, we got full cooperation from the Gorkhas and Gorkha workers to accomplish our research study. We started our field work in early 2009 A.D. and completed the study in 2010. So, almost one year we took time to conduct the fieldwork at tea gardens and other areas of Darjeeling hills and Dooars. At first, we felt it really an impossible task but at the expiry of one year of our study, we were inspired and determined by our urge and finally we could complete the field study by the end of 2010.

Objectives of the Study

Off the two prime objectives of the present study, first one is to explore the contents pertaining to the marginalization of Gorkha tea plantation workers of Darjeeling hills in particular and India in general and secondly the marginalization of Gorkhas of West Bengal in general. It will indicate as to how the Gorkha community as a whole has been marginalized in India. Still another objective of the study is to evolve and establish the Theory of Plantation Sociology or the Sociology of Ethnicity for the academic world and the scholars who are interested to understand the ways and means of marginalization of Gorkha community in India.

2

Knowing Darjeeling, Darjeeling Gorkhas and Gorkha Tea Garden Workers

Globally, Darjeeling is very famous for tourism destination for both the Indian and foreign tourists. Hardly, Darjeeling is known for its tea industry which but produces orthodox tea of international standard that is rather best known for each and every country of the world. Conceptually, Darjeeling is mostly understood to be as good as Nepal even by the Indian metropolitans. Whenever, we visit the metropolis, people ask us whether Darjeeling is in Nepal and there we have to make them understood that Darjeeling is very much in India. It shows that there is a distinct image of Darjeeling among the people of the country in particular and foreign countries in general. We think that our Indian scholars have not so far been able to make understood the global communities that Darjeeling is very much in India. It shows that Indians have not been able to make Darjeeling theirs or they have failed to mainstream Darjeeling on the political map of the country. Of course, politically, West Bengal and Bengalis of West Bengal try to forcefully keep Darjeeling within the political map of the state without integrating the people of Darjeeling with the mainstream society of the state. Integration also attaches the sentimental and emotional assimilation of communities for the commonality of interests. Keeping forcefully Darjeeling in the political map of West Bengal, what West Bengal is doing is that it is highlighting the colonial divide and rule policy as of the British colonialists. Do the Bengalis really know about Darjeeling and the people of Darjeeling? Certainly they could not do so, keeping in view of the articulated gap in integration methodology by the Bengalis of West Bengal in relation to the Gorkhas of Darjeeling hills. It is apparent from Kolkata and Siliguri centric development process of Government of West Bengal that reflects their ethnic progress by undermining the progress of other minor communities of the state.

If the Bengalis of West Bengal have very poor knowledge about Darjeeling hills, how can they comprehend the significance of people and tea industry of hill Darjeeling? Without knowing the region, how can they claim Darjeeling theirs—is a sad story of marginalization of Darjeeling hills along with the people thereof. We can call it as the rape of Darjeeling. How many Bengali scholars have fair knowledge of the history of Darjeeling, Darjeeling tea industry and the people of Darjeeling hills? In fact, objectivity of the history of Darjeeling has been buried in the interest of chauvinistic Bengalis of West Bengal. History of Darjeeling has been distorted and fabricated by the scholars who mostly belong to Bengali community. In fact, neither the Chowgels—the kings of Sikkim who claimed Darjeeling theirs, had fair knowledge about the real political map of Darjeeling (Pin: 1986) nor the people of Sikkim prior to the coming of British expansionists- imperialists in Darjeeling region. In fact, the land of Darjeeling was the bone of contention between Sikkim and Nepal kings since time immemorial. But ethnically, linguistically, culturally, economically and emotionally, both the Sikkimese and Nepalese (Gorkha) had common history, physiology, philosophy and geography. The living in hills had generated a kind of softness in culture among all the people of Sikkim and Nepal. The common sentiment/ emotion of the people of the two countries made them relatives, friends and co-dwellers in the Himalayas. The selfish nature of plain people especially made them harsh in course of time in the history of the region. Otherwise, still we found simplicity, innocence and sentiment among the Gorkhas which have now become weak points for themselves to be exploited by the Bengalis of West Bengal in particular and Indians in general.

Talking about the Darjeeling frontiers where tea plantations are located, it is found that Bengalis claim Darjeeling theirs but question is this that what they have done to make Darjeeling theirs historically. The tea plantations along with the entire hills were either the exploration of British people or created and flourished by the Gorkhas. What contribution did West Bengal and Bengalis made to Darjeeling is the pertinent academic question to the Bengalis in order to claim Darjeeling as the integral part of West Bengal. Had Bengalis really interested to develop Darjeeling and own Darjeeling on their fold then where they were then and now and what they were and are are doing for Darjeeling? In fact, as Bengalis belong to *Suvidabadi* (opportunist/comfort loving) community, they hardly participate in making any land habitable with other communities rather they occupy the suitable habitats made by other ethnic communities whom they in course of time make marginalized. They therefore, appear to be the exponents of the exploitation of marginalized communities for their *Subida* (comfort). This may be the reason why they always talk about their *Subida* and *Subida* (comforts) only. Dwelling on absolute comforts and compatibility to comforts made them the exponents of exploitation of other communities. It shows that Darjeeling was confiscated by the Bengalis for their comforts.

Tea Plantation Land

Whatever the tea garden land that is there in Darjeeling hills and Terai of Darjeeling district they had brought under the Tauzi Department of Government of West Bengal under the rule of Land and Land Reforms Department in 1956 simply because of the fact that Touzi land gives crores of rupees in every thirty years besides the agricultural tax and excise duty on Orthodox tea of Darjeeling hills. Whatever the revenue that is being earned from the tea plantations of Darjeeling hills is sufficient to meet the expenditure of West Bengal at least for six months of the year. It indicates that if the revenue earned from Touzi land tax and other taxes earned from the tea can easily meet almost five years expenditure for Darjeeling hills alone. Sociologically, now every Bengali hypocritically states that no more Darjeeling has that beauty of the past but alas why they want to keep Darjeeling and

Darjeeling people with them forcefully. Almost fifty thousand acres of land of Darjeeling tea industry can help to earn golden eggs every year for the West Bengal government. This might be the apparent reason why their poet, Rabindranath Tagore has called Darjeeling as their head and therefore called Darjeeling as Sonar Bengla (golden Bengal). The Darjeeling tea garden land itself was confiscated by the West Bengal government. Where is the logic to own tea garden land of Darjeeling district by the Government of West Bengal? Again, at the Sociological parlence, there is nothing common between the Bengalis and Gorkhas of West Bengal. Of course, Bengalis belong to ruling class and Gorkhas the ruled class in West Bengal. Now, they want to forcefully integrate hill people with the mainstream of Bengal but keeping Darjeeling isolated from the development packages and without peoples' participation with the mainstreams of West Bengal. In fact, they do not know anything about the Darjeeling tea industry and people who had shed blood and sweats to the tea garden land. Simply the Bengalis are the political experts to divide the Darjeeling people into groups who are alrady marginalized and bankrupt intellectually in so far as the propagation of genuine political consciousness among themselves and thereby establishing the communal unity is concerned.

This is apparent from the proposal that West Bengal Government and people thereof have made to make Siliguri sub-division of Darjeeling district as a separate district so that Darjeeling hills would be once again completely isolated and marginalized. Almost all the incentives, facilities and schemes of government have been concentrated at Siliguri on the one hand and Kolkatta on the other. The Kolkatta centric development strategy has ample impact on Siliguri of North Bengal. In fact, Bengal wants to make Siliguri another Kolkatta. In this way, operationally, the Bengalis themselves have proved the fact that Darjeeling has separate political entity having separate ethnic community. In this way, Darjeeling is simply the colony of West Bengal where the land belongs to colonizer and people of the land as the marginalized stock of isolated Darjeeling enclaves. The enclave concept of tea industry under British planters has been conceptualized in terms of tea garden land as well as the entire hills of Darjeeling. Darjeeling has been simply made as tourist destination of cheap Bengalis, middle class Indians and rich foreigners.

The land of tea industry of Darjeeling hills, if you go there and properly smell then you will find the scent of blood and sweats in it of the Gorkha workers like Man Bahadur, Dil Bahadur, Shyam Bahadur, Lal Bahadur, Hari Maya, Kaili Raini, Sahili Damani, Kali Tamangni etc. etc. There is no scent of any Bengali blood and sweats except the hegemony of post independent Bengali planters/managers. Like the British Government, the West Bengal Government has been simply protecting the so-called Bengali managers and bureaucrats at Darjeeling for the sake of its vested interests as mentioned above in the earlier lines of this chapter. What they have done for the socio-economic development of tea garden people including the people of Darjeeling hills since independence to to-day?

Today, the Government of West Bengal claims the tea garden land belong to West Bengal but not the people. Rather it says that they are immigrants or descendents of immigrants from Nepal. If it is so, why the government could not identify the Nepalis among Gorkhas to be the Nepali citizens of Nepal instead of its presumption formed ever since the independence that Gorkhas belong to Nepal. It is all about the political gimmick of the government because if this proposition has been materialized by the Government of West Bengal then even the present Chief Minister of West Bengal Government along with the majority of people of West Bengal has to go back to Bengladesh because they are also immigrants at West Bengal. So, the question of calling only the Gorkahs as immigrants means to marginalize the Gorkha community of Darjeeling along with all Gorkhas of India. The Government of India has also very poor knowledge about the ground realities of land as well as people of Darjeeling hills. This may be the reason why once Subash Ghisingh, the leader of Gorkha National Liberation Front called Darjeeling as "No-Man-Land". Where is the statistics of government of West Bengal that can show the exact number of immigrant population of West Bengal because every body has voter identity card, ration card, bank passbook and what not. Simply articulating phobia among the marginalized communities can not suffice the day except proving the malaise attitude of the Bengali community and Government of West Bengal. It would be rather best to call the tea garden workers as the owners of land of tea gardens as per Marxian philosophy to which the West Bengal Government is very much concerned. This may be the reason why the Himalayan Plantation Workers Union of GNLF wanted to have land deeds of the workers quarters and kitchen gardens. The concept of land to the tillers of the Bengal Government and people of Bengal is to be materialized if Bengalis want to prove that they belong to revolutionary community of the world in so far as the interests of peasants, workers, poors and marginalized people is concerned. Why historically, the Bengalis consider the Darjeeling hills as part of Sikkim and why not the integral part of West Bengal because there is no documented history of North Bengal including Darjeeling hills of the pre-British era. Rather, there is apparent history of the region under the rule of House of Gorkhas of Nepal in the region from 1780 A.D. to 1816 A.D. To be very specific, Bengalis do not have any commitment to Darjeeling hills, culture and people because they do not have any commonality of living in relation to their way of life with the people of hill Darjeeling. Talking about Darjeeling of West Bengal makes them boastful in front of other people of the country and abroad. But hardly any other community of the country knows the process of colonization of Darjeeling by the Bengalis and West Bengal Government. They due to their high level of hypocrisy and political power have colonized the hill land of Darjeeling by marginalizing the people thereof.

Understanding the Gorkhas

The Gorkahs have been made marginalized under the process of colonization of Bengal due to their Sakuni Niti or Chanakya Niti being accredited by the Government of India and Indian communities. Secondly, Gorkhas do not have unity among themselves. Thirdly, the Gorkhas though warlike people for the global communities, they are simply cowards for their ethnic cause as they hardly argue for the interest of their community openly and objectively. There is hardly any sense of unity among Gorkhas for pursuing any common goal. It is found among the Gorkhas a crab habit—pulling down the person who strives to move upwards or tries to acquire leadership. Whosoever, the big shot Gorkhas including the Gorkha bureaucrats are working for the government and other non-governmental organizations of West Bengal and India, they can simply be called as Shields (*Moharas*) of Bengali community, Bengal Government and Government of India. Every Gorkha is self-centered for himself, blind followers of mainstream political parties and operationally under the inherent poverty in so far as their way of living in the country is concerned. Sincerity to the ethnic cause is simply at the emotional level rather than at the realm of ground realities. The Gorkhas are ardent followers of other communities whether in social, economic, cultural or any other aspects of their life is counted. Encountering the agonies of life, an individual Gorkha himself has to evolve solution and the solution lies with Bengalis to whom he becomes again and again marginalized. This is the history of Gorkha ethnic community in West Bengal in particular and India in general. However, counting our experience in India, it is found that no other community of the country wants to extinct the Gorkha community but to make the Gorkhas half stomach community always surviving for their benevolence or *Subida*. Use and throw the people of the Gorkha community is the basic attitude of Bengalis of West Bengal. The moment their interest is filled up, they throw the Gorkhas into dust bin. If any Gorkha having its community supports, wants to do something genuine for the community, he is either purchased by the Bengalis or Bengal Government, if not, Bengalis instigate the local Gorkhas to finish him up to death. This is the history, ever since the independence of the country of the so-called Gorkha political luminaries of Darjeeling hills including

Subash Ghisingh of Gorkha National Liberation Front and even Bimal Gurung of Gorkha Janamukti Morcha—present agitating party of Darjeeling hills for the formation of the state of Gorkhaland in India. The Bengalis praise the Gorkhas till their interest is fulfilled and throw out to hell on the moment when their interests are accomplished.

Knowing the Gorkhas and Gorkha Tea Plantation Workers

Basically, the Gorkha tea plantation workers of Darjeeling hills are peripherals even to the eyes of local urban Gorkha community and mainstream communities of the country. In this context, we would like to cite the observation made by local scholar, Bidhan Golay who observes that knowing Gorkha at this present phase of globalization is very crucial and full of contradiction. He stated that the present phase is characterized by the interplay of two seemingly opposing and yet complimentary forces of essentialism and hybridity. At the one end of the continuum, it is a growing tendency in global political and economic forces towards greater integration on that is stoked by the continual movement of people and their cultural baggage across the boundaries of nation-states, throwing up new forms of trans-national practices, locations, solidarities and institutions that do not strictly confirm to the demands and logic of the nation-state. At the other end of the same continuum, still newer forms of micro-politics have secured moral legitimation, marking a distinctive shift towards the fragmentation of cultural landscape.

The old identity concept has been eroding very

fastly giving rise to new identities. Amidst the scenario, the crisis of identity of a community is now increasingly seen as part of wider process of change which has been dislocating central structures and processes of modern societies. In this situation, the Gorkha identity in India spanning the period of over two hundred years is found to be in continuing crisis. Golay further stated that the problem of identity is due to modernity. The modern identity is the symbolic boundaries of nation mediated by the complex discursive structures of national culture and national identity. Till now, by Gorkha, people understand in term of a community having Martial race charater and another is community having deterritorialized identity encircled by nationalism. It indicates either Gorkhas have to stick to the concept of nationalism imposed by other mainstram ethnic communities of the country or to struggle always for the ethnic identity. It means marginality of the community character and thereby oppressed and dispossessed. Not a single research study ever conducted by urban based mainstream communities has really been able to look and analyze the Gorkha community of the country objectively. Subjectivity is the orientation of the scholars—both the British colonial and post colonial who have lead to the misinterpretation of the Gorkha community. Their studies have highlighted the exclusion process of the Gorkha community in the country. They have defined Gorkahs as an exclusive ethnic group and thereby marginalized group of the country whose participation in the nation building contribution is to be thoroughly accountable.

Whether their participation in the mainstream socio-economic-political processes has been made any difference to the mainstream communities of the country or not; nobody knows. It is because of this reason, the comprehensive study of the contributions of social and cultural movements in Darjeeling and elsewhere towards the formation of a distinct Gorkha identity still eludes us. Whatever the studies so far have been done by the scholars, they are all tended to revolve around the celebration of the famed "bravery" of the Gorkhas. But the question is that for whom their bravery is utilized? The answer is for others and others only and not for own community.

The award of bravery given to Gorkhas by the British people still lingers and followed by other communities of the country. It is therefore, time has come to state that the Gorkhas are no more the believers of Hard Ware (Bravery) with *Khukuris* (community weapon), but Soft Ware (pen- diplomatic culture as given by the Bengalis of the country). Boasting on Bravery means to make Gorkhas prone to colonizing by other communities of the country. Talking about bravery means to accept the old concept of marginality of the community and making Gorkha community as mercenary force of the global communities. Another thing is that now the Gorkhas should leave the habit of showing fear psychosis or being marginalized and colonized in the mainland of West Bengal since Darjeeling is not for the Bengal alone but vice-versa.

For Gorkahs, whether Darjeeling is with Bengal or not, it does not connote anything different because for Darjeeling-Dooars Gorkhas in particular or India in general, Darjeeling Bengal is like Gorkha Proverb *"Bhira Bara Lare Pani Kilo Ritay, Bagha Lae Kahay Pani Kilo Ritay"* meaning thereby Darjeeling Bengal makes no difference for Gorkhas. The compositeness of the Gorkha community is itself the example of integration having many socio-cultural sub-structures and sub-layers. Historically, it is seen that the British had their own interest to recruit Gorkhas in Indian British Regiment just to cut into sizes the Hindus Brahamanical rites and prejudices in India as Gorkhas have mostly tribal characteristics shaped by the isolated Himalayan traditions. British lacked footsoldiers and cannon fodders for their wars of expansion in nineteenth-twentieth century. The Gorkhas being a warlike impoverished tribe fitted the bill well. They fought along with British in India, Afghanistan, Burma, Malaya, Libya, Egypt, Mesopotamia, Italy, France, Germany and all over the world where the British fought wars. Even in present-day Af-Pak region the Gurkhas are fighting alongwith British in war against Taliban and Al-Qaida, without involvement of Nepal or Indian governments. The British still possess Gurkha regiments in their army. The same background is also found till today to keep the Indian Gorkha Regiment just to curb so-called separatist tendencies and forces of the country. Otherwise, since Gorkhas are defined in terms of immigrant, isolated, marginalized and brave community, why India cannot disband Gorkha Regiment? It is the main reason, why India has kept Gorkha Regiment. If not, since Gorkhas as unwanted citizens of the country being looked down upon by the mainstream communities, how their bravery is essential for them. It is therefore simply to be called that Gorkhas are made for "use and throw" by all Indian communities of the country as per their requirements.

As the British colonialists did, the Indian colonialists

also have branded the Gorkhas simply as Fighting Race of the World and therefore in India also. The parameter set forth by colonialists both British and Indian to the Gorkhas is to be called as the Warlike Race of the world. This warlike race attracted may western countries to keep the Gorkhas in their countries. Everywhere, people are fond of the Gorkhas. Many British Indian Gorkha soldiers were forcefully married by the German ladies aftermath of the Second World War in Germany. But interestingly, such Bravery of Gorkha soldiers was not awarded at par with the British officers. A clear cut demarcation had to be made between Gorkha soldiers and British officers in terms of pay, promotion and in fact the whole question of status in British Gorkha Indian regiment and the same thing is also found today in Indian Gorkha Regiment. All the high officers of the Gorkha Regiment are hailed from the mainstream communities of India and Gorkha soldiers are made simply to be innocent, stupid, committed *(Nun Ko Sogo Garnu)*; to be simply the disciplined and dedicated soldiers of the country. Who does not scared of a Gorkha soldier? Even the race like Punjabi, Muslim and other communities also scared of the Gorkha soldiers in India for their bravery. This bravery is responsible factor for not realizing Gorkha identity in our country. Not to become coward for others causes and docile for one's own community is the real malaise of Gorkha community of the country. Civilizing and normalizing the martial characters of the Gorkha soldiers by the British Government in India is equally applied for the Gorkhas as whole in the country today through the state political power and sovereignty.

Whoever, prominent or intelligent Gorkha citizen

tries to agitate for the Gorkha identity, he is easily purchased by the political system of the country. Therefore, the question of Gorkha identity is at the level of discussion and not in practical realization. Every Gorkha is hungry of leading modern way of life by sacrificing everything of the Gorkha identity. This is the apparent reason why Gorkha intellectuals, bureaucrats and big sorts are simply the Shields (*Moharas*) of the mainstream political systems. Simply they are living for their affluent way of life undermining every other things of their identity. It may apparently appear to be objectionable to the Gorkhas subjectively but if we see objectively, it encompasses hundred percent ground reality. The poverty is the main factor both historically and present day consumerism of globalization that make the identity of Gorkha community lesser and lesser in orientation in our country. Whoever Bengali fomented the Gorkhas to realize their ethnic identity ultimately involves centrifugal mainstream community interests and finally sidelining the main issue of the Gorkha identity. Being hungry of the situation, every Gorkha forgets his ethnic identity easily and thereby makes himself ultimately marginalized at the hands of the same Bengali.

History of the Gorkha identity movement is the history of seeking political alternatives and this in every time leads to intra-community conflicts and blood shade upon which the mainstream communities become deligent and utterly happy as they can easily divide the Gorkhas into groups, factions and sections of antagonistic types. This is apparent from the time of agitation under Gorkha National Liberation Front and today's development between the Gorkha Ganamukti Morcha and Gorkha National Liberation Front in

Darjeeling. In both the situations, the Government of West Bengal and Bengalis of India are very happy as they can easily crack down the Gorkhaland Movement lead by earlier Gorkha National Liberation Front and present Gorkha Janamukti Morcha. It indicates that **Seeking Alternatives** is the history of Gorkha Identity movement in India. Gorkhas at one point of time try to go with a particular political party and again at another point of time with another political party in search for better alternatives. The main point to seek another political alternative in course of time is due to the Sakuni chauvinistic politics of Bengalis that involves cheap Jatibadi Niti of West Bengal. Lack of confidence among the Gorkha themselves and the domination of colonial capitalism on which the Gorkhas become prone to be messed very easily are other factors for their marginalization. This proneness to money and thereby participating in corruption practices is still another responsible factor for not realizing Gorkha identity by the Gorkhas in India over the last two hundred long years.

Comprehension of the distorted Darjeeling history is an historical accident committed by the mainstream scholars of the country in particular and Bengal in general. Basing on the simple oral term interwoven with myths and anecdotes that is passing from one generation to another is most unfortunate part of the story. Everyting written so far on the history of Darjeeling or knowing Darjeeling is mischievous efforts by the scholars hailing from other communities. The very blemishness of calling Gorkhas as immigrants by the mainstream scholars has not been challenged by the local scholars rather they go as per others' versions about us which is hundred percent wrong. It is a political gimmick rather than the absolute truth to talk about the question of Gorkha immigration in India. In fact, no present Bengali belongs to West Bengal, they all came from the Bangladesh. So, where is the efficacy to call only the Gorkhas as immigrants from the mainland of Nepal. If Bangladesh is reality for Bengalis, then Nepal is also the same reality for Gorkahs especially from the point of the history of socio-cultural dimension of the community is concerned. It is blamed that Gorkhas immigrated to the land of Darjeeling from Nepal due to push factor as "poverty" and pull factor as "*Munglan Ma Paise Falcha*" (India gives money to Gorkhas) is simply wrong orientations. If it is so, why the Bangladeshi Bengalis had immigrated to the land of India especially at West Bengal since Partition of Bengal (1905) and Bengladesh War of Liberation in 1971? This is the question to be pondered on by the present day Bengalis of West Bengal. Their proneness/ affinity to Bangladeshi culture, *Illish Mach* (most preferred fish of Bengalis) etc. makes them affiliated to cultural tradition of Bengaladesh and the same is also the truth with the cultural foods of Gorkhas being borrowed through their socio-cultural traditions from Nepal.

Culture does not limit geographical boundaries rather culture does not have any boundary. It can travel across the world. The Kali Puja and Durga Puja done in U.S.A. by the Bengalis is a glaring instance. The cultural softness of Gorkhas to be tolerant, patience, perseverance, committed, sincere, dedicated are not their weakness but symbols of Gorkha identity and Gorkha impression that were inherited from their traditions. Instead of doing this, the mainstream communities of the country treat Gorkhas as immigrants and immigration is used as a favourite stick to beat the community on most occasions. In this way, the history is tinkered endlessly with an intention to pass some kind of retrospective judgement on a community which makes the matter more confusing and hazier (Golay: 2010).

The report of British travellers including Dr. Campbell (First Superintendent of British Darjeeling) stating that there were 100 souls in 1839 at Darjeeling is no more an acceptable contention for Gorkhas (Pradhan: 1991) may be it is the fake base for Bengali scholars as well as other Indian scholars because how Dr. Campbell knew entirely the then geographical boundaries of Sikkim, Darjeeling and even Kalimpong within his tour of merely an year or two in the region. Did Dr. Campbell know the entire population of present Darjeeling District, certainly it is impossible in terms of ground reality. Certainly he did not know the entirety of Darjeeling hills. Did he know the importance of "Old Gorkha Station"? When it was constructed, why it was constructed, who constructed the same? No, never, since he was concerned then only with ruling and establishing Darjeeling town and not concerned with the Gorkhas separately and also the entire Darjeeling District. Every census was manipulated in British time and post colonial periods of history with reference to Darjeeling. Who wrote census? The Colonialists and Colonialists only and not by the local Gorkhas; Who could make colonialists the masters in the region, both British and Indians as easy way to rule and establish their political hegemony at Darjeeling. Making census is simply to manipulate figure in favor of ruling communities of the country as the same is found at Darjeeling also.

This is possible through adopting theories and administrative practices while dealing with the marginalized frontier people of North-East India. Gorkhas have and had purchased by the mainstream political system to inform the Census team to call themselves as people immigrated from Nepal, Sikkim and Bhutan or otherwise they would be put on trouble. The same thing is also found today among the immigrant Bengalis from Bangladesh in North-East India in order to cast votes in favor of ruling party for example in West Bengal ever since the last three decades of Communist rule. The narrow frontiers of North Bengal along with North-East India with Nepal, Bhutan, Sikkim, China and Maynmar apparently allow mainstream people to confuse and entertain conflicts among the people belonging to Gorkha community so as to affiliate Gorkhas adequately with specific country like India. The same thing is also found in case of Darjeeling. The frontiers know no geographical demarcation. The Gorkha community had been ruled by the concept of taming culture of the tea garden Coolies in Darjeeling and elsewhere in India. Just as the Gorkha soldiers, simple and free of religious prejudices was better suited as tea garden and other manual jobs that call for hardworking. The hardworking Gorkhas became very loveable to all communities of North-East India including Darjeeling hills. The colonial capital transformed the docile and hardworking hill men into a proto-wage labourer both in Darjeeling and other parts of North-East India. The agrarian pursuits especially terrace cultivation and Grazing land became the popular pull factors for shfting geographical loyalty from one place to another by the Gorkhas in North East India. We cannot say it immigration but shifting geographical loyalty of the Gorkhas. It is because of the fact that Gorkhas are very much prone to cosmopolitanism in so far as their mobility in the Himalayas and around the world is concerned.

Knowing the Gorkhas, we must say on the basis of our Siliguri experience where majority of people are Bengalis during the last thirty years that a Gorkha hardly believes another Gorkha in so far as the question of confidence creation among themselves is concerned. Of course, they talk about Gorkha identity but they do not articulate solidarity. It is because of the fact that the Gorkhas do not have Organic Solidarity simply we have Mechanical Solidarity and Mechanical Solidarity is as good as Negative Solidarity in the period of Globalization. The moment we feel of community identity we talk about this for the time being and thereby we instantly forget the issue and very easily we become the vendors of Bengali community. The Dalal culture as the symbol of the Gorkha community leads us to marginalize ourselves today. This is because of the fact that hybridization culture of globalization is easily as well as highly comprehended by Gorkhas rather than the identity realization of community and this is the present status of our identity movement in West Bengal. We can be easily made ourselves hybridized to other cultures.

Presently, Divide and Rule policy of mainstream communities of West Bengal through Sakuni/Chanakya Niti to Gorkhas is working well in the field of making respective caste-community organizations, religious affiliations, Scheduled-caste/tribe status earning endeavors so as to get government facilities by which they all the Gorkhas are weaken and divided and the mainstream Bengalis as British people did, can divide the Gorkhas easily and rule the Gorkhas as in the past. This is how we can know ourselves and Darjeeling and tea plantations in Darjeeling hills. In fact, why mainstream scared for Gorkha unity is due to the historical background and the background is related to the invasion of Sikkim, Garhwal and Punjab by the House of Gorkhas of Nepal in 18th century. The Sugauli treaty of 1816 and Indo-Nepal Friendship Treaty of 1950 have made the Indian Gorkhas marginalized, isolated and neglected human resource stock of the country like India.

Coming to the question of marginalization of Darjeeling Tea industry, it can be said that the end of Darjeeling tea industry will help to restore the Gorkha identity because at least then the West Bengal Government may not have hegemony to the region by making the region a *Sona Ka Anda*. The earlier colonialists were white coloured British and now the present colonialists are black coloured Bengali Babus at Darjeeling. The black coloured Bengali Babus look Darjeeling with the same lenses as did by the British people. British used to talk about Gorkha identity fakely and again black Babus of Bengal Government very often also talk about the Gorkha identity fakely for realising their interests rather than the interests of the Gorkha themselves. In this way, now and then the issue "Gorkha identity" is defined, raised and discussed by the black coloured Bengali Babus of various walks of life of the West Bengal. In normal time, Bengali Babus inspire the general Gorkhas about realising Gorkha identity as the same did by Shri Jyoti Basu, during 1950 to 1980 but the same Bengali Jyoti Babu rejects the issue of Gorkha identity later on when the Gorkhas as a whole become volatile to the cause of

Gorkhaland as the symbol of Gorkha identity during 1984-1988 in Darjeeling. Bengali polemics and political dialectics is hard to understand by non-Bengali Gorkha people. They sometime give one signal and some time another signal, which is very confusing for layfolks. From this perspective, at least, we the unbiased scholars from our Gorkha community should thank the Bengali community for making alive the Gorkha sentiment and Gorkha identity movement ever since 1955 to today. This has however left the impression that Bengalis do not have long term vision realizing the implication of what they say at one point of time and another which helped to have rampant ethnic movement in Darjeeling as well as North Bengal ever since the independence of the country.

Industrialisation in West Bengal

The West Bengal Government talks about industrialization of North Bengal especially at the tea frontier which is the greatest economy of North Bengal. But pondering on the *modus operandi* of tea industry of the region, it is found today that the government is simply involved in luring process of making revenue from Darjeeling tea industry by undermining the problems of the workers who make tea for their colonial interests. This is apparent from the fact so far that the Government of West Bengal having almost two hundred years of tea garden industrialization in North Bengal which alas could not even established Minimum Wage Board for the workers. Simply sustaining the organized exploitation of the workers through tripartite agreements, the Government of West Bengal has became the prototype of marginalizing the tea plantation workers of North Bengal who are either Gorkhas or

Adivasis and both the ethnic communities have been still called immigrants or descendents of immigrants. Not a single tea plantation worker is by ethnicity Bengali.

The West Bengal and West Bengali community having Sakuni Niti/Chanakya Niti is in fact, the responsible factor for the denudation of Industrialization process in West Bengal. Community politics can not sustain the industrialization process which rather calls for the dominance of universal culture rather than the community culture to dominate the industrial relation issues of the workers. Whatever the strike politics so far undertaken by the West Bengal Government are proved to be political rather than the labour-based (Rawat: 2010). This is the reason why industrialization has become a distant dream for West Bengal today. On the one hand, the Government of West Bengal pursues the policy of industrialization and on the other hand, the strike politics just to collect votes at the time of elections and this has made antithetical the whole process of industrialization. The workers are their party pet dogs who can be used as sincere working class of the plantations in normal time and wariors at the time of realising their political mileage. There is nothing sort of the existence of plantation workers in so far as achieving their better and progressive living is concerned.

Trade Unionism Today in Darjeeling Hill Tea Gardens

Trade union according to Ramanajum (1986) as Honey Bee for the industry has become poison today for the industrialization process of West Bengal. It neither attracts the attention of industrialists nor the interests of the working class of the industries. The same picture is also found in case of Darjeeling tea industry where the local trade unions are simply misguiding the Gorkha tea plantation workers to fight for their sectional interests. The management of the plantations is very happy to purchase only a few central leaders of trade unions keeping in hell the rank and file workers of the plantations. The issue like Bonus of the workers attracts the attention of trade unions along with the purchasing capacity of management of the plantations. How to make workers uninformed with the total fact is the holistic technique of both the management and trade unions of tea industry of West Bengal. Let them be in darkness is the technique of both the management and trade unions so that partly unions can exploit the workers and partly management and partly by the government officials who are associated with the issues of tea plantation workers. They say to the workers that the workers do not know wide official formality relating to industrial relation processes and paraphernalia. Whatever the agreements on industrial relation issues are done at either Kolkatta or Siliguri appeared to be the top secrets between the unions and management. If any rank and file worker asks for details, then he will have to be excommunicated from the plantation or beaten to his death. Secondly, the Government of West Bengal wants that let the unions hailing from hills go to hell by fighting against each other. Since 71.0% of tea plantation workers are females whom the union leaders and management personnel can easily lured with whimsical assurances of better living with better facilities tomorrow but interestingly tomorrow hardly sees the light of the day. Trade unions appear today simply the horses of their political parties rather than the protective organizations for the workers. Therefore, the trade unions have become philanthropic organizations of a few union leaders rather than the organizations of rank and file tea plantation workers. To the workers, union leader means the political leader who is to be considered as *Thulo Manche* (big sort) whom the rank and file workers can not question on any issue pertaining to the workers. The criminalization of trade union politics being followed from the political party through unofficially declared manifesto has really put low participation of rank and file workers in trade union activities today in the era of globalization. All the consultations, discussions, agreements and sharing of gains of collective bargainings between the management and unions are done in either big hotels or at the secret places so that nobody from the rank and file workers can understand anything about the contents of discussion and agreement. The same old system of making workers under the reductionism is the process of industrial relation agreements in the industry. Every stakeholder of the industry is busy with just to realize its sectional interests. Having majority of women tea plantation workers who remain busy with their household chores do not get time to think about the issues pertaining to them. So far, not a single woman trade union leader of high ranking is found in tea plantation industry of Darjeeling hills. Everything of the trade unions is monopolized by the male folks who are not mostly the real tea plantation workers or who belong to tea plucking category of the plantations. Not a single permanent supervisory or clerical staff is normally appointed today by the tea garden management. Only temporary or contractual labour appointment is given today. Here in this context, unions remain silent as they are purchased by the management of the industry. Not a single house is repaired today as workers themselves have to maintain their houses. Whatever the facility provided like ration, fuel, medical, drinking water etc. as per the provisions of Plantation Labour Act, 1951, they all appear to be just the ritualistic in orientation and not complete in realisation. Every worker is busy with his own interest as to how more and more money can be earned within short span of time because they do not have any more confidence on tea industry and the sustainability of tea industry for ever in the region. Discussing about the Provident Fund of the workers, it is seen that hardly there is any tea garden in Darjeeling which regularly deposits the provident fund of the workers to the office of Provident Fund Organization of Government of India. Again, on this issue, unions are found literally silent. One of the points to be noted here is that instead of knowing this why the workers join processions, strikes etc. called by the respective political parties? It might be due to the racial character of Gorkha tea garden workers who rather enjoy with warlike situations, violence and untoward incidents which we believe is due to the martial character and Bhul Bhulaiya nature of the Gorkhas. Otherwise, they, by heart and soul, know that they are again going to be cheated by unions by involving them in such procession or struggle. It indicates their level of innocence, simplemindedness and sincerity to political parties. It shows that Gorkha first knows political parties and then their Gorkha community while Bengalis know that at first they are Bengalis and after that only they are the followers of respective political parties. This is the mark of great difference between the Gorkhas and Bengalis as observed by these scholars ever since their thirty years of living at Siliguri of West Bengal. It means that the Gorkha tea plantation workers are there today where they were in 1955 doing truly the trade union movement in Darjeeling when at least ten Gorkha tea garden workers, mainly the women and children were shot down by the then West Bengal Government police.

The Gorkha trade union politics is the politics of political parties while the trade union politics of Bengali community is the politics of Bengali chauvinistic politics of West Bengal. For the name sake only, the Bengali trade union leaders talk about trade unionism but their *modus operandi* of trade unions appeared to be perfectly the community-based rather then tea garden working class-based today in the period of globalization. They are very good harbinger of hypocrisy in true sense of the term that they talk high about the welfare of working class of the plantations but alas the results as we have looked are opposite on comprehension. This is transparent from the closure of fourteen tea gardens of Dooars area of West Bengal and present pitiable conditions of the closed tea plantation workers of Dooars of North Bengal. In fact, the Bengal Government and the Bengal Trade Unions are all lead by the Bengalis and Bengal Government officials who have made very good vicious circle because it is the vicious in the sense that their affinity and association have impacted by the negative results to the tea industry of region in particular and Darjeeling tea industry in general. The economic unionism of the West Bengal trade unions have proved themselves to be the economically self-centered entities rather than centering themselves around the cardinal interests of the workers and industry. Simply tea plantation workers work in the plantations for secondary source of income while it was primary source of income of the workers in the past till 1991. Almost 73.0% of Gorkha tea plantation population are dependent upon outside income (Sharma: 2009) source as their family members are working either in various parts of the country or abroad. If it is the bare reality of the situation, how can we expect to have the holistic commitment of the workers towards the tea industry of Darjeeling-Dooars and North East India?

Talking about the policy of Divide and Rule of West Bengal Government, now we experience a deep animosity being established by Bengalis of West Bengal between the Gorkha and Adivasi tea garden workers at Dooars- Terai region of West Bengal. Doing this, the idea of West Bengal Government and thereby the West Bengal Bengalis is to weaken the Gorkhaland movement lead by the Gorkha Janmukti Morcha in Darjeeling hills, Terai area of Darjeeling district and Dooars region of Jalpaiguri district of North Bengal. To get hoid of the lost of past political grips of West Bengal upon the Gorkhas and Adivasis is the prime objective behind pursuing political gimmick. The illiterate, innocent Adivasis are being fomented wrongly against the Gorkhas so that Bengali communal politics can sustain for ever in the region.

In order to do so, even some Gorkha vendors are also being utilized by giving some ransom that can help the Gorkha vandors a lot for the time being. Articulating permanent solution to the problem can not be expected from such Sakuni/Chankaya Niti of the West Bengal Government. Deconstruct the internal social structure of Gorkhas by means of fragmentation of the same is the sole objective of Bengalis today so that the political structure of the Gorkhas can be broken into pieces and that is the basic idea behind this political gimmick of West Bengal Government.

Dearth of Research Studies on Indian Gorkhas

Neither any body nor any organization of the country is serious about conducting the objective study of the Gorkhas in India. The Gorkhas appear to have been the subjects of marginal interest of the country. Operationally, they are given the status of second class citizens in the country. The Gorkhas of West Bengal particularly the hill areas of Darjeeling district are looked down upon with suspicious eyes by the Bengalis. The struggle done to establish Darjeeling and other towns by the Gorkhas have all gone to astray. Making the Darjeeling land habitable and then sold out to others is the characteristic feature of Gorkha community. For example, once in Siliguri, most of land was owned by the Gorkhas prior to the merger of Darjeeling district to West Bengal during the British time but in course of time the Gorkhas either sold out their land to the Bengalis and other ethnic communities or confiscated by the Bengalis themselves and now the Gorkhas are called immigrants from hill Darjeeling and North-East India. Hardly any objective study has been done so far about the Gorkhas of Siliguri sub-division, Dooars and other North Eastern states of the country.

Thus, an objective research study of the Gorkhas of Terai and Dooars as well as North-East India is actively needed today because there is an absolute influence of Gorkha culture, society and tradition in the region. The present study does not take into account of the fabricated social history of Gorkhas ever written by the outside scholars or scholars belonging to other ethnic communities of the country. This is the noble effort of the present sociological enquiry on Gorkhas of the region.

Being Gorkhas by ethnicity, we can assure the readers that they will smell Gorkhness in each and every aspect of socio-cultural, economic and political life of the people of the region. Let the scholars be sincere enough with their job while writing anything about the Gorkhas of the region. If they do not perfectly know about the Gorkhas, why they are pursuing to misinterpret the social history of the region? Without knowing the social history of the Gorkhas, how they are writing about the Gorkhas? This is a note of caution given to the Bengali scholars to be particular while writing anything about the Gorkhas today. We, the scholars have been pondering on to explore the reasons why Gorkhas have been marginalized, exploited and made peripheral in North-East India? Exploring the reasons, it is found by us that the martial character like, stubbornness, sincerity, commitment and deterritorialization of Gorkhas are responsible factors for marginalizing the Gorkhas in India. Fortunately, the Nepali/Gorkha language helps Indian Gorkhas to come to a common platform of social intercourses. Otherwise, there would have been no Gorkha as such today in India. This is spectacularly found in case of state like Assam, Nagaland, Mizoram, Manipur, Meghalaya, Tripura and Arunachal Pradesh where all the Nepalis/Gorkhas speak together in Nepali/Gorkha language. Nepalization or Gorkhali acculturation process is simply flourished in India rather than in Nepal where respective caste/tribe still speak its own dialect. The sense of Gorkha Nationalism has been formed in India (Subba: 2008) only. Linguistic homogeneity is the characteristic feature of Gorkha community in India. These scholars had the opportunity to work in Arunachal Pradesh where there are still 82 tribal groups. The Gorkhas are mostly preferred for agricultural revolution in the state of Arunachal Pradesh along with other states of North-East India. There are still some tribes in North East India who prefer to pursue on shifting cultivation rather than the settled cultivation. But here too, the tribals who are having Gorkha neighbours speak Gorkha/Nepali language and vice-versa. When we were officially working in Chowkham area of Lohit district of Arunachal Pradesh, we could see it very apparently between the Gorkhas and Khampti tribe of the Chowkham, Wakro and Medo areas of Lohit district. Nature loving character of the Gorkhas helps themselves to adjust with the local tribes of Arunachal Pradesh, Mizoram, Meghalaya, Nagaland, Tripura and Assam. Yes, it is found that the other ethnic groups like Bengali, Bihari, Marwari etc. are also there in North-East India but they are mostly concentrated in towns and Bajars only and they are mostly found to be engaged in business and service sectors of North-East Indian economy. Along with the local tribal dialects, Nepali is also widely spoken by these business communities of North Eastern region of the country.

3

The Gorkha Tea Garden Workers

Apparently, the existence of Gorkhas is found from the Mahabharata days in India. The Gorkhas as every body knows are famous for their martial character which means they were mostly engaged in Indian militia. But hardly Indian mainstreams have fair idea about the fact that the Gorkhas are equally competent and contributory factor for the emergence and growth of tea industry in North East India. Darjeeling tea industry has in fact, sustained the world famous tourist destination and for this, the tea gardens have beautified the tourist destination with permanent greenery. The greenery through tea gardens has helped the significance of Darjeeling tourism industry. This may be one the reasons why the Government of West Bengal instead of having nostalgia to the people of Darjeeling wants to keep Darjeeling within the political map of West Bengal. The Gorkha tea garden workers are the custodials of this greenery because they keep the gardens green and worthy to look at and enjoy marvolously. The inherent history of their shifting loyalty to tea garden jobs from agrarian pursuits is due to their nature loving character in which pursuing on floriculture is one of the most important orientations of Gorkha way of living everywhere in the country and world. They apparently love and care forests and forest resources and they love every greenery at home and neighbourhood. Sustenance of green tea bushes at Darjeeling hills is due to this praiseworthy character of the Gorkhas. Darjeeling flora and fauna as maintained by the Gorkhas is still famous in the world.

This common habitation of tea gardens as of the agrarian niches of countryside was the pull factor for Gorkhas to join the tea garden jobs. The same greenery, the same forests and in fact the same habitat made them easily adjusted with tea garden universe of Darjeeling hills. The British planters could know the emotion, sentiment, culture and society of the Gorkhas. The clear comprehension that the British planters had about the Gorkhas could perfectly help them to prosper the tea industry in Darjeeling hills. The Sardari system of labour recruitment was only the means of bringing labours at tea gardens of Darjeeling. But the process of recruiting the labours was luring at the places of origin and then followed by indenturing and pursuing captivity of the labour force at the gardens. Having mostly the tribal background of their places of origin, the workers made the tea garden universe theirs putting blood, sweats and sorrows. The hope for better future living at the gardens made them optimistic throughout the history of almost two centurion years of living at Darjeeling tea plantations. The Gorkha tea garden workers of Darjeeling hardly asked the managers and Sardars for their rights. It was Late Shri Ratanlal Brahman, the local Gorkha leader who inspired the workers to fight for their rights after 1943 in Darjeeling. Every day, the workers were tame to go to Mela (duty place) in time and come back straight to their home from the Mela and hence they were not allowed to know anything about the outside world nor any new person of the outside garden. Even they had to seek permission of Sardars to attend sick family members at the hospitals. For the social issues like marriage, death rituals and education of children, they had to approach to Sardars and get approval from the planters/managers. If they did not do so, then they would be ousted from the boundaries of tea gardens under the *Hatta Bahira* system. Such captivity process of the workers was accorded to the tea gardens managers by the British Government. Captivity was the alpha and omega of tea garden working population in the region during the British and post independence periods till 1991.

Emergence of Social Organisations and Trade Unions at Darjeeling Tea Gardens

With the birth of Gorkha Association in 1907 and NEBULA (Nepali-Bhutia and Lepcha)—an amalgamated social organization of Nepali, Bhutia and Lepcha in 1920, Gorkha Dukha Niwarak Sangh in 1932 and the emergence of Gorkha League Party in 1943 as well as the Communist Party of India in 1946 in Darjeeling, the tea garden workers started participating slowly in the processions and secret meetings held at the Labour Dhuras of Darjeeling tea gardens at night and thereby coming to the outside world of tea gardens. Mobilizing the tea garden labour force was a big problem for the people who wanted to enlighten the hill tea garden workers. However, at that juncture, the British planters started playing well with a new card and that card was ethnicity card to play for sensitizing the Gorkha tea garden workers to claim for the separate Gorkha identity in West Bengal so that the workers and their leaders did not disturb the modus operandi of tea garden enclaves. In this way, the British capitalism was however remained undisturbed at tea industry of the region till independence.

After the independence of the country, the British planters started capitalizing the interests of Government of West Bengal and through the Government of West Bengal, they tried to sustain the same Planters Raj (Guha: 1977) in Darjeeling even up to 1955 when about ten tea garden workers were killed by police firing at Margrete Hope T.E. of Darjeeling and that was the era of penetration of trade union movement at Darjeeling tea gardens. But here at this juncture too, the local trade union leaders like Ratanlal Brahmin, Ganeshlal Subba, Bir Bahadur Hamal etc. could have to play the fabricated drama under the directorship of Shri Susil Chatterjee—a Bengali by ethnicity who had his ample communal trade union interest at Darjeeling tea gardens on behalf of the then Bengalis and West Bengal Government.

Shri Susil Chatterjee could have been beaten every card of trade unionism by himself at Darjeeling tea gardens on behalf of West Bengalis had there not been the cultural differences of hill tea garden workers from rest of the West Bengal Bengalis. So, he had to forcefully delegate his power of trade unionism to hill Gorkha trade union leaders and thus in 1946, Darjeeling Cha Bagan Mazdoor Union was formed. In the meanwhile, the regional political party known as Gorkha League Party also formed a union known as Darjeeling Chia Kaman Shramik Sangh. Interestingly, both the unions had local Gorkha leaders which attracted the attention of tea garden workers to be associated with the unions and fight for their rights as industrial workers of tea industry of the region. In the same manner, under the leadership of Smt. Maiytree Bose, National Union of Plantation Workers (NUPW) was formed with the political banner of Congress Party of India during the sixties of 19th century. Similarly, with the formation of Darjeeling Gorkha Hill Council in 1988, another trade union known as Himalayan Plantation Workers Union also emerged for tea plantation workers of Darjeeling hills under the banner of Gorkha National Liberation Front party. Further, in 1995 again, under the leadership of Communist Party (Revolutionary) Marxist of India—the splinter of Communist Party (M) of India of West Bengal, the Darjeeling-Terai-Dooars Plantation Workers Union was formed. With the coming of Gorkha Janamukti Morcha, another trade union for the plantation workers known as Darjeeling-Terai-Dooars Plantation Labour Union had been formed in 2009.

The above description shows that every time, the Gorkha tea plantation workers have to seek for Alternatives but every time, they are cheated with the Sakuni Niti/Chanakya Niti of Government of West Bengal and by the Bengalis of West Bengal. It is because of the fact that ultimately the mighty political power lies with the Bengalis and West Bengal Government right from Darjeeling to Siliguri to Kolkatta to New Delhi. The New Delhi always take into due cognizance of the proposals of West Bengal Government which is consisting of Bengalis only whenever any issue of marginalized communities of West Bengal comes to the fore of Indian Parliament. Whenever, the Gorkhas including the Gorkha tea plantation workers are given a small piece of bread, they become very very happy but they do not have fair idea as to how big slice of the bread is being consumed by the Bengalis and the West Bengal Government for the specific issue. In the name of national integration, every time the Gorkhas have to sacrifice everything for the benefits of Bengalis and West Bengal Government—nobody knows the totalitarian facts.

The formation of Mahakuma Parisad at Siliguri was the result of Sakuni Niti/Chanakya Niti of West Bengal Government to isolate Darjeeling hills from the plain area of Darjeeling district. Here, in this endeavor of Shri Ashok Bhattacharjee, the Municipal and Urban Development Minister of West Bengal Government, Shri Subash Ghisingh, the supreme leader of the then Gorkha National Liberation Front, remained almost silent as he was being made pet dog of West Bengal Bengalis. Almost all the important government offices had been transferred from Darjeeling to Siliguri with the patronage of West Bengal judiciary and executives as well as ministries of the Government of West Bengal. Every Gorkha of Siliguri was in oblivion while the Gorkha leader was enjoying with all lavishness and aristocratic way of life at Darjeeling hovering round the Delhi, Mumbai, Benaras and other cities of the country and even foreign countries just to kill his potential time.

One after another, whimsical issues were thrown before the Gorkha Public of Darjeeling through the political agenda of his GNLF party just to confuse the Gorkhas of Darjeeling hills. Sometime he talked about No-man's land issue, sometime cultural revival issue like Jhankri festival, Devi festival and so on and so forth. In this way, interestingly, every time, right from 1946 to today, the Gorkhas as well as Gorkha plantation workers had been completely made fool.

But here, we would like to put an enquiry as to why every time the Gorkhas as a whole become the victims of the dirty games of the political parties? May be, it is due to their simplicity, lack of political consciousness, semi-literate society and martial character. Every time, they know the consequences of violence but still they prefer to easily involve in the violence. The martial behaviour is responsible factor for being fools by the political parties, they involve on violence due to the desire of the political parties of the region. Even culturally, the Gorkhas are followers of various religious sects, systems and pet dogs of various ethnic communities. Not a single Gorkha openly criticizes the West Bengal Government at Siliguri. Every time, they appear to be scared of the Bengalis and the West Bengal Government.

Now, is therefore appropriate time for the Gorkhas to say that they are absolutely different from Bengalis—socially, culturally, economically and politically. What is there in West Bengal for Gorkhas? Everything is being owned and monopolized by the Bengalis. Forcefully, the Gorkhas have to accept that they also prefer *Maach* (fish) like Bengalis do while there is no fish culture as part of food habit among the Gorkhas rather they like to have *Gundruk, Kinema, Jhar (Tongba), Rakshi, Sinki* etc.—all are the fermented foods. Talking about the vegetables, *Raya Sag* (mustard oil leaves), *Ghyu Simi, Iskosh Ko Jara* (quash roots), *Churpi* etc. are really loved items borrowed through tradition by the Gorkhas. These are the cultural realities of Gorkhas in so far as their food habit is concerned. For example, we being the Gorkhas do like to have Mutton prepared in Gorkha fashion with outer skin of the he-goat while Bengalis do not like to have the same. So, where is the cultural similarity and affinity between the Gorkhas and Bengalis in so far as their food habit is concerned?

Cultural Softness of the Gorkhas

The Gorkhas always keep adequate softness (calling others *Bichara, Bhaiya* to Bengalis, Marwaris, Biharis and others), sincerity, stubbornness, commitment, dedication and sacrifice for the cause to whosesoever the job is meant for. They have own manner to address others with respect, own jester to entertain others while flourishing the interpersonal relationship. The attitude carrying respects to others of the Gorkhas as well as their smiling faces are their inherent cultural images and identity symbol whereas the Bengalis hardly smile in their day-to-day life.

This is the queer experience that we got living with Bengalis at Siliguri for the last thirty years. The cultural softness of the Gorkhas might have been considered as the weak point for marginalizing them selves in West Bengal in particular and India in general. We have forced to narrate the queer story because we have been messed by the Bengali intellectuals including our own teachers at the University of North Bengal which we have already mentioned in earlier chapters of the study. By the "cultural softness" or cultural software, here we mean the kindheartedness which we found mostly among the Gorkhas while other communities of the country particularly Bengalis do not have such cultural softness. A Bengali becomes very happy if his friend is in awesome position in any day of the life. Every Bengali criticizes his intimate friends and vice-versa which is rarely found among the Gorkhas. If a Gorkha does not like his friend then he left the friend and does not entertain any relationship from tomorrow. This is, of course, an inherent weakness of Gorkhas not to have ethnic solidarity. Ethnically, all the Bengalis instead of having lots of differences, come to a common understanding when anything goes wrong against their Bengali interest in West Bengal or India. For example, today talking about the formation of Gorkhaland, all the Bengalis of the country are in one platform irrespective of political, religious and economic affiliations and prove themselves first they are Bengalis and then they belong to Congress Party or Communist Party or Trinamul Congress Party or Bharatiya Janta Party etc. In this way, the Bengali community is very communal, conservative and cosmopolitan.

Their cosmopolitanism is reflected through their *Subidabadi* culture. *Asubida Hulo*—having little bit uncomfort is unbearable for every Bengali. Thus, lack of cultural softness is the characteristic feature of Bengali culture which is directly opposite to Gorkha culture. Although a Bengali for his vested interest pays attention to another Bengali but the moment his interest is fulfilled he throws another Bengali on the dust bin. This artificiality is the apparent way of life of the Bengalis. A Bengali becomes very happy if another Bengali could not do *Subida* (comfort) with anything of the agenda. Helping another Gorkha openly in the presence of the Bengalis hardly matters among the Gorkha themselves at Siliguri in especially ordeal situations because he apparently becomes scared to do so may be due to the fact that he does not want to invite any problem to him later on from the local Bengalis. In fact, hypocrisy polished by artificial show ups is the Dronacharya Mantra of the Bengali cultural life. Giving false assurances, promises and favours to others are simply the way of life of the Bengalis of West Bengal because culturally they have made themselves bankrupts today. To have hypocrisy, every Bengali always thinks and plans but in most of the cases transparent result of such planning appears to be negative and destructive as well as biased. This is apparent from the socio-economic situation of present day West Bengal.

The West Bengal is nowhere today in India in so far as its socio-economic development is concerned. All the important industries including Tata group of industries have been shifted to other states of the country from West Bengal. Talking about the tea industry—the only industry of North Bengal, it is at the verge of total extinction. They talk about the industrial revolution in the state of West Bengal without having revolution on their mindsets and thought patterns. They are like this and therefore they teach other communities also in the same fashion. This is indicated by the creation of animosity between Adivasi Vikas Parisad and Gorkha Janamukti Morcha today in Dooars-Terai areas of West Bengal since both the communities have been living together at the region for more than three centuries. They have articulated the card of ethnic division between these two communities for their vested interest and the interest is to divide them and easily rule Darjeeling-Dooars/Terai with the dictatorial political will of the West Bengal Bengalis.

The Culture of Being Purchased

Right from the day of the birth of Gorkha League

Party in Darjeeling under the leadership of Shri Damber Singh Gurung, every political leader has been easily purchased by the Government of West Bengal. Exploring the fact, it was found that Shri Damber Singh Gurung was purchased with sixty thousand rupees and finally Shri Damber Singh Gurung had to leave the Gorkha League Party and joined Congress Party of India and won election and became the Member of Legislative Assembly of West Bengal in 1951. Same is the case with other subsequent leaders like Ratanlal Brahmin of Communist Party (M) of India, Deo Prakash Rai of Gorkha League Party and other Gorkha political leaders from Darjeeling.

However, Shri Subash Ghisingh of Gorkha National Liberation Front could make hardiest challenges to West Bengal Government but finally Shri Ghisingh was also being purchased by Mr. Jyoti Basu, the then Chief Minister of West Bengal with as heavy weight as possible ransom in 1987 only. However, Shri Subash Ghisingh lingered the Gorkhaland agitation till 1988 just to make the Gorkhas of Darjeeling-Terai and Dooars tired in such a fashion that whatever afterwards he intended to do as a pet dog of West Bengal, nobody would dare to object him thoroughly or actively. The smell of purchasing job is also found with Gorkha Janamukti Morcha leader, Shri Bimal Gurung and others as well as other political leaders of various regional political parties of Darjeeling today as the state Legislative Assembly election is at the doorstep i.e. scheduled to be held in April or May, 2011. It is also found that almost all the Gorkha political leaders of Darjeeling hills are always appeared to be hungry for money and money only. One positive point noticed since 1947 is that one group of political party of

Gorkhas earned good wealth and it is replaced by another group of next political party in power.

Interestingly, it is also observed that the West Bengal Government has the legacy of purchasing the Gorkha leaders every time in the political history of Darjeeling. Otherwise how an agitating Gorkha leader becomes silent in course of time when he becomes the de facto head of Darjeeling hills. Might be, he does not have dejure political power at his hand, but he intentionally messed the basic Gorkha identity issue for his personal interest by making a lot of pretensions and false agenda. Still some of the old people think that Darjeeling Gorkha Hill Council of Shri Subash Ghisingh is as good as Gorkhaland state for Indian Gorkhas. In reality, Mr. Subash Ghisingh had not even power to appoint a permanent peon in any office under his DGHC. Every time, the Bengalis and Bengal Government plays very easily the Gorkhas with the Gorkha sentiment, emotion and culture and think to purchase the Gorkha leaders with small piece of dry wheat bread. So, in the purchasing chess board, every Gorkha leader is being easily played with the Bengali chauvinistic politics of West Bengal. Claiming Darjeeling land along with all resources of Darjeeling appears to be the birth right of West Bengal and West Bengal Bengalis.

Whatever the efforts that are being done by the West Bengal Government are ultimately meant for the maximum benefits of the Bengalis of West Bengal by undermining the genuine problems of marginalized ethnic communities of West Bengal. They are simply interested with Darjeeling revenue and dictatorship at Darjeeling. To any extent, the West Bengal Government goes to exterminate the interests of

Gorkhas and Gorkha political leaders of the region. Again, it is also found that so-called Gorkha leaders learn Sakuni Niti/Chanakya Niti from Bengali Gurus (teachers) at Siliguri or Kolkatta and go back to hills to do dirty politics among the Gorkha brothers and sisters only because they cannot do the same cheap politics in the plain areas of West Bengal. This is how a lay man's conscience gathers experiences for almost half decade or till his death. The question is that how long more years our Gorkha leaders are being sold in the political market or Bajar in the same fashion. It shows that Gorkhas are more conscious about class position rather than caste and ethnic affiliation by heart in the strict sense of the term. They can be easily made lured, indentured as well as make slaves socio-culturally. Not a single Bengali believes Gorkhas today and vice-versa. A kind of cultural hatred has taken place between these two communities today in West Bengal. Yet the Gorkhas have not left the habit of following Bengalis in day today socio-economic life in the region.

This nature of Gorkhas is perfectly the culture and tradition of Himalayan tribes of India. If it is so, why presently Gorkhas of Darjeeling-Terai-Dooars of West Bengal have kept motive and desire to be called as tribes as acclaimed by Shri Subash Ghisingh of Gorkha National Liberation Front is an issue for thorough academic retrospection for the entire Gorkha intellectuals. Every Gorkha becomes very happy if he belongs to reserved category of the government may be due to the reason that his children would get government jobs and reservation in other spheres of socio-economic life. We have seen this even among the intellectual Gorkhas who become very happy if his caste is made Scheduled Tribe or Scheduled Caste in India. But during the earlier days, they had a deep allergics and annoyance to be called themselves as Scheduled Tribes or Scheduled Castes in the region. It indicates that the Gorkhas—the followers of Cow Dharma are not sure about their identity hovering in dualism of caste-tribe continuum (Srivastava: 1966). Now is therefore the appropriate time to call ourselves as either purely Gorkhas or simply the isolated tribes of the Himalayas. We have to first ascertain this in order to come to a concrete conclusion for fighting for Gorkha identity in India. The Gorkha identity should not to be merely at the gossiping level. This is indicated by the fact that today on the one hand the Gorkhas are fighting for Gorkha identity but on the other hand every Gorkha caste or tribe is busy to make communal caste/tribal organization stating that each caste or tribe wants to revert to original state of affairs. The marginalization process is within the community itself and after that only the Bengalis who always endeavour to study the darker sides of the Gorkha community, do easily marginalize the Gorkhas. Amidst the process, the Bengalis purchased the influential Gorkha leaders including the intellectuals with cheap alms with which the entire Gorkha intellectuals, politicians and bureaucrats appear to be very happy. This has created a binary classification of the Gorkha community into haves and have-nots in Marxian phraseology. Secondly, the marginalization game is played by West Bengal Government with the cooperation of urban Gorkhas of Darjeeling, Kalimpong, Kurseong, Siliguri, Dooars and Mirik who are absolutely mongers for money and money only so that they may have lavishing urban way of life.

For example, we have found that still the rural as well as plantation dwellers of the region are considered as backward stock of Darjeeling Gorkha community calling them as *Kamanees-Bustiwalas*. This carries a kind of inferiority complex among the people of *Kamans* and *Bustees* in Darjeeling hills. They can be easily purchased or cheated by the urban dwellers or town people of Darjeeling hills. It has also however, found that the talented people among the Gorkhas become the objects or commodities to be purchased by the Bengalis and West Bengal Government. Once in a blue moon, such Gorkha talents are recognized by the West Bengal Government just to make fake justification that they respect the Gorkhas as good as the first class citizens of West Bengal. How many Bengali Communists died for Gorkhas? How many Bengali Congress men died for Gorkhas? How many Bengali Trinamul Congress Party men of West Bengal died for Gorkhas? None of the Bengalis and never, while thousands of Gorkhas died for Communist Party (M) of India at West Bengal and Congress Party of West Bengal during their rule in West Bengal or in Darjeeling over the period of last six decades of independence. It is because of the fact that Bengalis do politics for the sake of politics only while Gorkhas do politics for the cause of political party keeping aside the respective ethnicity chores at dust bin. This is the weakest point of Gorkhas in Darjeeling in particular and India in general. They act as pet dogs of West Bengal to bite their own community people at the farthest end with unsustainable ransom. In the use and throw out politics of Bengalis, the Gorkhas have simply become cheap dogs to be purchased for their malaise political games. Our consolation towards the pitiable Gorkha conditions is due to our own life history at Siliguri ever since the last three decades on the one hand and our association with the Bengalis on the other. Simply we cannot make any Bengali a true and intimate friend. Here, if we make any Bengali our true friend than we may be definitely exploited bitterly by the same friend today or tomorrow or if not he will try to purchase us for his personal benefits. Bengali outwardly howsoever friendly may be in behaviour but reserves his deepest contempts for Gorkhas. Interestingly, now, the Gorkha political leaders have also learnt this as to how one is to be politically philanthropic and ardent exponents of hypocrisy that is normally to be poured upon the own community on behalf of the Bengalis of West Bengal as Bengalis know how to purchase the Gorkha leaders ever since 1947. Like Bengalis tried to divide and rule the Gorkhas, the Gorkha political leaders also very well know how to divide Gorkhas and earn bread and butter easily. Bengalis are a political community and they have mastered the art of politics at deepest level, other communities are new entrants to it and have to master the art of politics. It shows that the marginalization process is a holistic process of the Gorkha community ever since the time immemorial.

The Gorkha tea plantation workers of Darjeeling hills were first marginalized by their own caste/ community Sardars at the plantations followed by the marginalization process of British planters/managers and still later on after independence by the Bengalis of West Bengal through their government. If this is the reality of the Gorkhas, why should Gorkhas talk anything against others or other ethnic communities of the country in so far as the marginalization of Gorkha community in the country is concerned? All the beautiful, talented *Chelis/Naris* (women) of the Gorkha community come under the carnal sexual desires of other communities. The statement can be supplemented by the fact that most of the beautiful, educated Gorkha women have been married to either the Bengalis or other ethnic communities including the foreigners. This may be the reason why derogatorily we called Gorkha women as *Allu* (potatoes) which can be comfortably mixed with any other vegetables that give all time better and better taste. Later on in their life, the so-called Gorkha *Chelis* or *Naris* show nonsensical reaction for their mistakes committed in their lives without achieving any positive result. It is because of the fact that the time they realize the ground realities it would be too late to correct the same.

Gorkhas Today in Darjeeling Hills

The West Bengal Government is busy in making animosity among the Gorkhas at Darjeeling by dividing the followers of Gorkha Janamukti Morcha into different political parties including the revival of GNLF of Shri Subash Ghisingh who was ousted two years back from Darjeeling by the Gorkha Janamukti Morcha. Now within the Gorkha Janamukti Morcha party of Darjeeling also, divisions have been taken place with the Sakuni/Chanakya Niti of West Bengal Government headed by Shri Ashok Bhattacharjee, the Urban and Municipal Development Minister who happens to belong to Siliguri city and who is very busy since two decades to gallop with the process for Siliguri centric development. All the money given to Darjeeling hills has been spent at Siliguri and Siliguri only just to win election with Bengali votes. To dwell with the Sakuni Niti/Chanakya Niti is the birth right of present Bengali community of West Bengal. Ashok Bhattacharjee by heart and soul wants that let there be series of conflicts among the Gorkhas so that he can easily win the patronage of Government of West Bengal to tame the Gorkhas of Darjeeling and North Bengal in his favor. This is due to the reason that this time he has to face tough competition from Trinamul Congress Party at the state Assembly election which is scheduled to be held in early 2011 in West Bengal.

It appears from the political scenario of West Bengal that Shri Ashok Bhattacharjee and his party, the Communist Party (M) of India has remotest chance to get majority seats in West Bengal State Legislative Assemby. On the other hand, the Gorkha Janamukti Morcha appears to support the Bharatiya Janata Party might be its Member of Parliament, Shri Jaswant Singh, has assured GJMM to consider the issue of Gorkhaland in Indian Parliament. But, it is visualized today that the story will be same as it happened in 1980 when the local hill people supported CPI (M) leader Shri Joyti Basu who once inspired the Gorkhas at Kalimpong of Darjeeling district to demand for Gorkasthan.

But the Gorkhas could not understand the reality that Shri Jyoti Basu was first and foremost a Bengali and then the leader of Communist Party (M) of India. He exposed this fact during the Gorkhaland agitation when he killed thousands of Gorkhas in Darjeeling hills and finally he purchased Shri Subash Ghisingh, the leader of Gorkha National Liberation Front of Darjeeling and formed Darjeeling Gorkha Hill Council which functioned for two decades with his Sakuni

Niti/Chanakya Niti ignoring the election to be held to DGHC for four consecutive years that too out of the democratic political process. This was the immediate cause of the emergence of Gorkha Janamukti Morcha Party in Darjeeling hills in 2007 and thereby the downfall of Shri Subash Ghisingh. Interestingly, the same story is going to repeat again with the leadership of Shri Bimal Gurung today in Darjeeling when he has agreed to form Interim Council in Darjeeling. Only the point of confrontation between the GJMM and the Government of West Bengal is the mode of formation of Interim Council along with the map of proposed council. Here, GJMM wants the nomination from the party only while the Government of West Bengal wants it by multiparty election.

It is the contention of the Government of West Bengal that there are also other parties in Darjeeling such as Gorkha League, Communist Party (Revolutionary) Marxist, Bharatiya Janata Party and Congress Party. Every political party wants that it should get hold in Darjeeling so that the Gorkha Janamukti Party is slowly gone down into non-existence. It is visualized from the present situation at Darjeeling that in the state assembly election of 2011, the same story will repeat that had taken place in 1978 in Darjeeling hills when the then Pranta Parisad boycotted the election while the Gorkha League filed nominations through its candidates.

It may so happen that the Gorkha Janamukti Morcha—the present popular political party may boycott the election but other political parties will file nomination for their candidates. That will be the end of the story. Here in so far as the Interim Council is concern, ultimately the Government of West Bengal will use iron rod to conduct the election of the council with multiparty participation. This is most important speculation considering the present situation at Darjeeling. Here, it is found that every regional political party leader appears to be marginalized with the hands of Bengali politicians and West Bengal Government. Each hill political leader is busy to be played well at the hands of Bengali political leaders of West Bengal.

The Gorkha leaders come down to Siliguri or Kolkata and meet the Bengali political leaders who try to give Sakuni Niti to put down upon the another Gorkha political leader so that Bengalis can easily divide the Gorkha leaders of various political parties and ultimately rule Darjeeling very easily with mighty political power of West Bengal. This is the normal process of marginalization of Gorkhas by Bengalis ever since the independence of the country and therefore it will not at all be a new story for the history of marginalization of Gorkhas in West Bengal in particular and India in general. The nature of marginalization may be different in different states of North-East India but the process of marginalization is same all time and this is the overall history of Gorkha marginalization in India.

To know the Indian Gorkhas, one has to know Darjeeling Gorkhas who carry the representative image of all Gorkhas of India. What Darjeeling Gorkhas feel, do and act today, it affects the whole Gorkhas of India tomorrow and interestingly even the Nepalis of Nepal who are temporarily living in India and they also look it with the same lenses. The most important fault lies with the political system of India in dealing with

Gorkhas in India is that the Government of India along with the state governments of North-East India including West Bengal has failed to distinguish the Gorkhas of Indian origin from the Nepalis of Nepal origin. There is no mechanism to distinguish the same. This is also the same in case of Bengalis from Bengladesh today in West Bengal.

The Particularisation of Gorkha Plantation Workers

If the above described situation is with the Gorkhas as a whole of the country, just imagine the platitude of the Gorkha tea plantation workers of Darjeeling hills in particular. The particularization of Gorkha tea plantation workers can have a parallel to the Gorkhas as a whole. The Gorkha Tea plantation workers of Darjeeling hills are completely peripheral not only to the Government of West Bengal but also to the developed Gorkha community of the country. Tea plantation workers are some time made to be optimistic in realizing a few benefits and rest of the time to dwell on with pessimistic gesture leaving themselves in oblivion. What the management is doing, what the trade union leaders are doing and what the government officials are doing is almost hundred percent non-transparent to the workers. No transparency culture can come to the tea industry of the region. During the British period, Gora-Sahib-Coolie Raj was there and today Indian Kala Sahib-Labour Raj is on the vogue. Only the difference is that today Indian Kala Sahibs are there while in British period, there were Gora Sahibs as planters/managers. But the way of marginalizing the Gorkha tea plantation workers is same. How to make the plantation workers indifferent to the inherent secrets of the plantations is the main technique being followed by both the British and Indian tea plantation Sahibs. Even if some Gorkha Managers and Assistant Managers are there in hill tea plantations they are simply busy with their own interests because they know by heart and soul that they are simply pawns (*Moharas*) of the owners of the industry and the owners are all outsiders who want to squeeze as much as possible and leave the gardens by following the process of lockouts when they start to fetch low tea prices. Further, they invest the profit elsewhere the country in some other business because they are traders rather than industrialists in true sense of the term. This is all possible because 71.0% of tea plantation workers are females who do not mind to object this done by the owners and managers as they are mostly remain busy in the household chores after the *Mela* or garden duty. They do not get time to even think all about the industry and management as well as owners of the industry. It is observed that most of the female workers informed these authors as *"Kunai Jog Ayee Pani Kanai Chireko"* meaning thereby every owner or manager comes and goes with the same goal and the goal is to earn as much as possible within a stipulated point of time and gallop away from the plantations over night. In fact, no owner or manager has any kind of association to the place and people. How to earn more and more money as early as possible is the singular motive of the managers and owners. In this way, the plantation workers are made simply means to realize the sectional interests of stake holders of the industry and the stake holders are owners/ managers, trade union leaders and government officials. Doing this, it is found that the workers also do not keep deep commitment to the industry and therefore, the garden duty today is very much optional and not obligatory on the part of workers as in the past. If a worker does not like to go to *Mela* (duty) on any day of the month at the garden, nobody including the Assistant Manager or *Kamdari* can do anything except to motivate him or her to join the garden duty. So, the labour market in tea plantations as in other sectors of the Indian economy has become open that means thoroughly optional in nature and practice.

It is very difficult to get the work done through the workers by the management today in the liberalized era (Choudhury: 2000). *"Kaman to Kam Garnu Posaudaina"* meaning thereby, working in the gardens do not meet the daily needs of the workers' households. This may be the reason why most of the male members of the workers households opt for other kind of works rather than the tea garden jobs. Whoever the males are there in the industry as the clerical, supervisory and technical hands, they appear to be always not happy with the plantation authorities and this may be the reason why the unit trade union leaders do not do jobs accurately and to whom the management has to rather favour with extra income otherwise the clerical staff, office Babus, technical hands and supervisory staff would be annoyed with the management. So, what the managers normally do these days is that they try to make the clerical staffs, Babus, technical hands and supervisory staff happy.

Otherwise they will create havoc at the plantations. This is the inherent reason why most of the managers are always found to be intimate with the Babus including the Head Babus or Head Clerks of the plantations. In this way, the managers are able to marginalize the rank and file workers. To purchase these few hands is very easy but it is very difficult to purchase hundred and hundred workers of the plantations. It has also been heard from the workers that in very many matters there are specific earmarked percentage of share between the managers and Head Babus who check and pass the bills for payment, manipulate the bills and also make fake bills to be produced to their audit party or owners.

On the other hand, the tea garden owners are also happy to have substantial profits leaving the remaining profit margins to the managers and a few vested interest people of the plantations. Secondly, under the marginalization process, the managers purchase the most influential trade union leaders of existing party in power. For example, earlier at the regime of Gorkha National Liberation Front, Shri N.K. Kumai, the President and one or two other leaders of the then Himalayan Plantation Workers Union used to be purchased by the tea garden management with good ransom leaving the rank and file tea plantation workers as obedient dogs of the union leaders on oblivion. The same system except by giving a few new little incentives to the workers and staffs of the plantations by the Darjeeling-Terai and Dooars Labour Union of Gorkha Janamukti Morch Party, is sustaining well today in the hill tea plantations. Shri Roshan Giri, the President of the union is also the General Secretary of the GJMM party today in Darjeeling hills. Shri Roshan Giri hardly talks about the trade union movement but he always talks about the political movement among the plantation workers for the achievement of Gorkhaland state in India.

But in fact, he, by his heart and soul knows that there is a remotest chance to have Gorkhaland in India in near future also because he is the Junior Gorkha Sakuni among the Senior Bengali Sakunis of West Bengal. It indicates that Gorkha tea plantation workers like Gorkhas as a whole of India are simply pendulums of the various political parties, political leaders, trade union leaders and government officials of West Bengal. Similar picture is also found in other plantations of North Bengal and North-East India. One of the reasons for not having or permitting Gorkhaland state in India is due to the existence of Nepal which hardly talks about the problems of Indian Gorkhas to the Government of India whereas the Indian Government talks openly about the plight of Madhesis (people of Indian origin in Nepal) with Nepal.

This is still another reason why Gorkhas are marginalized in India. In fact, Nepal is wholly dependent on India in so far as its national life is concerned. Talk about economy of Nepal, talk about the transport and industry of Nepal or talk about the service potentialities of Nepalese citizens of Nepal, India is only the option. Medicine, doctors and other health services to Nepalese citizens are provided through India only. This is another root cause of the marginalization of Gorkhas in India. Realizing ethnic identity appears to be simply a myth for the Gorkhas in India. We would like to share our experience at Siliguri today. In fact, since our university life, we were the ardent supporters of Students Federation of India of Communist Party (M) of India but after the Gorkhas of Siliguri came under the grip of Gorkha Janamukti Morch of Darjeeling hills, even the persons like us have also been rejected by the Communist friends at Siliguri because they think that we have also shifted our philosophical loyalty to the Gorkha Janamukti Morcha. This is how every Gorkha whether he is Congress minded, or Communist minded or Trinamul Congress minded or other parties minded, has been branded to be the supporters of Gorkha Janamukti Morcha party of Darjeeling hills.

In fact, no Gorkha is now believed to be their benefactors, friends, followers as well as the well wishers of Bengalis today at Siliguri. Here lies the tragedy of Siliguri Gorkhas and Gorkha identity. Our identity has been questioned by Bengalis of Siliguri now and then. Of course, tomorrow when the problem will be settled, they will again try to bring the lost Gorkhas into their fold and we are sure that the same thing will happen tomorrow as it happened in the past after the Gorkhaland movement was over in 1988 in Darjeeling. And in this way, now and again Gorkhas will have to bow their heads down to the Sukuni Bengalis of West Bengal. The marginalization is the alpha and omega of the Gorkha community in West Bengal in particular and North-East India in general. The same story was there at Siliguri at the time of Gorkhaland agitation launched by Shri Subash Ghisingh during 1984-1988. Interestingly, from 1988 to 2008, all the Bengalis used to call Shri Subash Ghisingh as Ghisingh Sahib because Shri Ghisingh sold the Gorkha identity at the hands of Bengali community of West Bengal.

The Gorkhas of West Bengal are generalized as Bengali Gorkhas, thereby first Bengalis and then next the Gorkhas. The Gorkhas are for them the bonded slaves of modern age. If any Gorkha is excellent they claim their Gorkha friend as their state's communal property. This is indicated by the fact that good-educated Gorkhas are their human resource capital while ordinary Gorkhas are considered to be the state liabilities. The Gorkhas are called good friends of theirs or sons of West Bengal till Gorkhas are loyal dogs to the Bengalis but on the moment the Gorkhas become disgruntled and seek for identity realization, the same Gorkhas become their enemies giving them the status of immigrants from Nepal, Sikkim and Bhutan as well as North East India. This is the generic view of all Bengalis in West Bengal. This is how the Gorkhas are being marginalized. It is very easy to lure Gorkhas. For example, now the West Bengal Government is asking GJMM to ask any thing except Gorkhaland state. It means that till the span of six decades from 1947 they did not do anything to Darjeeling hills. Whatever they did, they did for plain Siliguri town only. The impact of such partisan approach of the Government of West Bengal and Bengalis of West Bengal is found at each and every aspect of the life of the Gorkhas. The impact is equally prevalent among the Gorkha plantation workers of Darjeeling, Terai and Dooars areas of North Bengal. Against this background let us discuss the marginalization of Gorkha tea plantation workers of Darjeeling hills, Terai and Dooars region of West Bengal as a case study to prove that how the entire Gorkhas of India are marginalized across the history of two hundred years.

4

Marginalization of Gorkha Tea Plantation Workers

The whole lots of marginalization of Gorkha tea plantation workers in West Bengal is the replica of marginalization of Indian Gorkha community right from the British days down to globalized era of 21st century. Therefore, the study has divided the period of marginalization of Gorkhas and Gorkha tea plantation workers into three phases, viz., British phase, post independence phase and globalized phase of 21st century. Discussing the marginalization, care will be taken to the very migratory nature of Gorkhas since time immemorial in the Himalayas. Secondly, marginalization will take into account of both intra-marginalization process and inter-marginalization process. Doing this, we will be able to really trace out the root causes and consequences of the marginalization of the Gorkhas as a peripheral entity in the country. Gorkhas shed their blood and sweats but mostly for others' rather than for their own. After 1816 at the end of Anglo-Nepal wars, the British realised their military value, their courage, steadfastness in adversity, stubborness and above all loyalty. More and more Gorkhas were recruited after 1857 rebellion, when British lost trust of many martial tribes and castes in India. They utilised Gorkhas in their wars of expansion and defence of imperial interests all over the world. Gorkha blood is sprinkled nearly all over the world where British fought. They fought in North-East India, North West Frontier, Afghanistan, Malta,Burma, Malaya, China, Singapore, Hongkong, Thailand, Boer War in South Africa, First World War in Turkey, Egypt, Mesopotamia, along with Lawrence of Arabia, and France. In First World War more than 2 lakh Gorkhas served. During the Second World War more than 2.5 lakh Gorkhas took part and fought in North Africa, Syria, Italy, Greece, France, Germany, Burma etc. They were in Falklands war with Argentina too. Currently they are fighting along with British in war against terror in Af-Pak region. For independent India Gorkhas' sacrifice is no less than of the Indians, right from 1947 war with Pakistan in Kashmir, they have fought with immense courage, bravery and sacrifice, in 1962 China war, 1965 war with Pakistan, 1971 Bangladesh liberation war, in IPKF against LTTE in Sri Lanka, and against terrorists of all hue till date. Gorkhas have won 26 Victoria Crosses, and three Param·Veer Chakras. What contribution could they do for their own ethnic identity of the country? While contribution of soldier Gorkhas is recognised all over the world and many books are available on that subject too, the contribution of civilian Gorkhas in building Indian economy is often ignored, and Grokhas being Himalayan highlanders, the mainland Indians always think that the Gorkhas are peripheral, mercenary, and therefore secondary in so far as their accountability to the country is concerned but central communities are always highlighted whenever anything special is done by any person of a mainstream Indian community. General Indian public thinks them as *bahadurs* fit for gatekeeping *chowkidari* persons only. Gorkha diaspora is spread all over India and in many parts of the world. Being peaceful, docile and law abiding citizens, they seldom create any trouble in their area of habitation/occupation, so they seldom make any news or create any newsworthy affair. The same story is found in case of Gorkha tea plantation workers of the region. The other working communities of the tea industry like Adivasis have Jharkhand, Bihar, Orissa and Bengali Babus of plain tea gardens of West Bengal have their respective states in India but the Gorkha tea plantation workers along with the whole Gorkhas do not have any state in India. The Bengalis, whenever they talk about the West Bengal, they talk about Kolkata but whenever Gorkhas talk about themselves, they have to talk about Darjeeling as the place for realization their Gorkha identity. It indicates that Darjeeling is the place of preference for Gorkhas as the Bengalis feel only Kolkata to be the appropriate place for their identity realization and not the whole of West Bengal. It indicates that the Indian Gorkhas are closely associated with Darjeeling. Every Gorkha of the country knows about Darjeeling by name or the importance of Darjeeling by heart. Whenever any Gorkha talks about Darjeeling, they feel proud of the same as the Bengalis feel proud of talking about the Kolkata only.

Marginalization of Gorkhas During The British Period

During the British period, the Gorkha tea plantation

workers of Darjeeling hills were treated as *Kamanee Coolies* living under the complete sovereignty of Gora Kaman Sahibs assisted by ignorant Sardars and Gallawalas who used to lure their respective caste and tribal workers from the agrarian belts of Darjeeling, Dooars, Terai, other places of Eastern Himalayas and even very few workers from Nepal. Of course, the marginalization of Gorkha plantation workers was very transparent and nothing was there to hide and seek in the process of marginalization. Each Sardar used to get one paise per worker every year from the Kaman management as recruitment, administering and monitoring allowance. The Gorkha caste and tribal Sardars used to be very happy with the *Bakhshis* given by the Gora Sahibs. Rather the Gorkha Sardars used to think fortunate to get the post of Sardars at the plantations. Not only the Sardars used to do the above jobs for the Gora Sahibs but even they used to supply beautiful ladies at the Gora Sahibs' bungalows if the Gora Sahibs wanted to exploit sexually the beautiful ladies of the plantations.

Although the Gora Sahibs used to appear as British gentlemen here at the plantations they were sent to open and run the plantations considering them as anti-social elements in England, Scotland, Ireland and other European countries. The plantation workers had no say in so far as their socio-economic and cultural life was concerned till 1947. But such behaviors became a rich legacy for subsequent independent Indian neo-colonial planters and managers. Even up to the present globalized era, the managers and owners used to think that the tea plantations as their colonies or estates where they were to be the sole kings and workers were tought to be the slaves of the Indian Sahibs. The binary social structure could be seen at the plantations between workers—the stock to be always suffered from inadequacy on the socio-economic frontiers of their life while the management—the stock having lavishness in all respects of their life. Good bungalows, faithful servants and full luxury made the managers really kings of the tea estates. The plantation workers had to seek permission in each and every aspect of their cultural life. To have a marriage of daughters or sons, the workers had to seek permission or approval from the managers. Whatever the managers used to tell was to be taken as final. Nobody dared to talk against the managers at the plantations. *"Hukum to Jawab Chaina"* meaning thereby there would not be any counter-argument against the orders of the managers as we have then found in British Gorkha Regiment in India (Munglan). It means that there was no question of industrial relation between the management and workers.

The work of workers was the subject of the management being dictated by planters' whims. The freedom movement for independence of the country could not penetrate deep into the tea plantations of Darjeeling hills. Rather the British managers lured the Gorkha tea plantation workers later on to involve in the ethnic identity movement. Weekly *haats* were only the source of exposure for workers within the plantations being approved by the management of the plantations but the businessmen who used to come down to the plantations for their day's business had to go back to Gundri Bajar (Darjeeling) in that evening only.

The planters had kept North Bengal Mounted Rifles

to beat, banish, control and thereby manage the so-called savage tea plantation workers at the plantations. If any worker could not be controlled by the Mounted Rifles, he used to be ousted from the plantation along with his family members under the *Hatta Bahira* System. Such *Hatta Bahira* system was prevalent at Darjeeling plantations only throughout the British period and in some cases up to the late sixties of 20th century in Darjeeling. The most important feature of British Planters' Raj was the existence of full discipline and sincerity at the plantations which are hardly found today. Thus, the period is called as the period of taming the Tea Plantation Coolies. Tame and tame the Coolies appeared to be the apparent management philosophy of the British planters. A horse, hat, and hunter *(chabuk)* were part of the personality of British planters. The managers who could not tame the Coolies were considered as useless and not fit for the job. Gorkhas had no Mai-Bap-father and mother in so far as their working at the plantations was concerned. If anybody talked anything against the planters' system, they were called Communists and managers used to motivate the rank and file workers that those Communists would spoil their future and families and therefore they should not hanker after such Communists. Amidst the situation, late Shri Ratanlal Brahmin started mobilizing the tea plantation workers since 1940 at the tea plantations of Darjeeling hills. He was attempted to kill by the British planters and administration but failed because he got the supports of tea plantation workers of Darjeeling hills. At that time, Shri late Ratanlal Brahmin had no preconceived notion that he was also working hard for the ultimate benefits of Sakuni Bengalis of **West Bengal**. He appeared to be the viable alternative for the then tea plantation workers who thought that Ratanlal Brahmin (Mahila Bajee) would save them and liberalize them from the age old British slavery. In this way, late Shri Ratanlal Brahmin became the Masiah or saviour of the workers. One of the interesting things among the Gorkhas is that at first, they make a particular person as Masiah or saviour and later on they abruptly became rude to finish him up to his death. This is the story of the Gorkhas in so far as their political consciousness is concerned. Late Shri Ratanlal Brahmin was worshipped in such a fashion that he became the Member of Legislative Assembly of West Bengal from Darjeeling and further later on, the Member of Parliament during the government of Shri Jyoti Basu as Chief Minister of West Bengal.

Thus, the marginalization process of Gorkha tea plantation workers during the British period was found with both the British planters and Bengali revolutionary Communist leaders. In simple term, the then Bengali community as a whole had mostly no fair idea about the growing hegemony of Gorkhas in Darjeeling. Thus, marginalization was then the one way traffic of British planters. Such marginalization process was patronized by the then British Government. The plantation workers during the British period could be easily called as mercenary force of the tea estate economy. The greatest damage done by the British marginalization process of the Gorkha tea plantation workers is that still their legacy is prevalent among the Sakuni Bengalis of West Bengal to marginalize the whole Gorkha community of the region. For the interests of West Bengal Government and Bengalis, the tea plantation workers have to act like slaves, of course, in not overt but covert form.

Marginalization during the Independence Era

Once the process of marginalization had been established at Darjeeling tea plantations, the same process of marginalization was followed later on by the Indian tea planters and managers at Darjeeling. Only the technique of marginalization was different. The tea plantation workers of Darjeeling became simply the vote banks of the Congress, Gorkha League and Communist parties. The only point of difference was that the Gorkha tea plantation Coolies had given the status of tea plantation workers after the independence of the country. With the formation of various trade unions, management associations and the introduction of tripartite and bipartite conciliation systems on the industrial relation issues of tea industry, the tea plantation workers became the subject of organized exploitation by the stake holders of the industry. Therefore, the tea plantation workers suffered due to the process of organized marginalization process at the hands of management, trade unions and even to some extent the government officials. Instead of having two hundred years of history of Darjeeling tea industry, the Government of West Bengal could not enact and implement the provisions of Minimum Wages Act, 1936. This may be the obvious reason why today the Government of West Bengal is planning to form Minimum Wages Board for tea plantation workers in West Bengal. It indicates that the tea plantation workers are not regulated by the provisions of Minimum Wages Act, 1936. While active and militant trade unionism was encouraged by Bengali leaders in West Bengal, but in Darjeeling Hills reverse was allowed to happen.

In the name of bipartite and tripartite negotiations,

the tea plantation workers are being marginalized both within the community and outside by the West Bengal Government and Bengalis of West Bengal. The marginalization process was articulated stating that the social cost of production was very high to be given to the workers. The low productivity of labour was considered by both the tea garden management and Government of West Bengal to be the main cause for the decline of tea industry in West Bengal. This has resulted into the emergence and growth of management–union rivalries that lead to the reccurrences of rampant strikes and lockouts in West Bengal tea gardens during the independent era. Here purchasing of trade union leaders was only the option left to the management of tea industry and it again lead to the emergence of distrust culture in tea industry. Each stake holder of the plantation was busy with its own interest keeping away the interests of the rank and file workers. Of course, they knew as to how the rank and file workers could be made fool. They knew this technique from the Sakuni Bengalis of West Bengal. Every Gorkha trade union leader became hungry of ransom from the management of the plantations.

This is how the Gorkha rank and file tea garden workers were marginalized during the independent era. Nothing tangible development could be taken place for the development of tea plantation workers in West Bengal and Darjeeling hills during the post-independent period. Thus, the period can be called as Period of Dirty Politics of the stake holders of tea industry. The period can also be considered as the era of trade union rivalries having respective interests of political parties, militant trade unionism and crafty politics of the management and owners/traders of tea industry of the region. Here the role of Government was the role of a helpless child having very weak regulating government mechanisms for the same or ineffective mechanisms of the Government of West Bengal.

Marginalization in the Globalized Era

With the adoption of Globalization, Liberalization and Privatization policy by the Government of India in 1991, everything went on changing. The structural adjustment process under the policy of government equally affected the tea industry of the region. The adjustment process started affecting all the stack holders of the industry and also the working class of the industry in an adverse way. All the trade unions now have to be defensive unions by leaving the habit of offensive entities as in the past and management became the exponents of hypocrisy stating that the industry remains always at loss. Here, the workers are of the view that if the industry remains always at loss why the owners are running the industry? It is obviously a very pertinent question ever put forward by the workers in the globalized era when every body knows that Darjeeling orthodox is sold at very high price at the international market. Yet, the tea companies of Darjeeling tea industry do not show actual figure of profit earned from the plantations.

Therefore, it is presumed that marginalization of workers would be there till the tea companies start showing the accurate figure of interests that they are earning. This can never be taken place in future also. The trade union leaders also do not have fair idea about it. Simply they say that workers are marginalized and exploited but they do not have the actual facts and figure about the profit structure of Darjeeling tea industry at their hand. In this way, our Gorkha trade union leaders are also marginalized by the management and owners till today in the period of Information Technology. Even Darjeeling Orthodox tea by way of blending is being marginalized in the global market although the Tea Board of India is trying to rectify the fallacy committed regarding the blending of Darjeeling Orthodox Tea. The acceptance of Fair Trade policy from U.S.A. has not make any difference to the Gorkha tea plantation workers as the workers are not being brought under the provisions of Fair Trade policy. Neither the Bengal Government wants to leave the tea industry nor does it do anything good for the tea plantation workers of Darjeeling hills. In fact, with mighty political power, the Government of West Bengal wants to marginalize the workers along with the entire Gorkhas of Darjeeling hills, Dooars and Terai areas of West Bengal. Marginalization as a holistic approach of West Bengal has been also accepted by the Government of India.

Coming back to the question of Gorkha identity, today, the political parties of West Bengal are trying to bring the Gorkhas of Darjeeling in their fold without doing anything. The Gorkha Janamukti Morcha of Darjeeling hills is simply interested to have Gorkhaland Regional Authority at Darjeeling hills. The sole motive of West Bengal Government and thereby the Bengalis is going to be fulfilled again by the political marginalization process of Government of West Bengal, Government of India and Gorkha Janamukti Morcha.

It appears from the recent political eventualities at Darjeeling that once again all Gorkhas of the region are going to be marginalized. The globalized era has completely allowed the Bengalis to marginalise the weaker sections of the society, community and backward-poor people very beautifully. The marginalization is the process of exploitation by a majority group over a minority group in the country. Only big communities have their upperhand in decision making process along with the formation of specific policy. In fact, all the communities including the Bengalis scared to have Gorkha unity.

The marginalization of Gorkhas in India is all time history of then social evolution. All the communities of India especially mainstream communities are ruling classes and minor communities are the ruled classes in India. If Gorkhas are united then the entire country will be on the fold of Gorkhas—it is the only preconceived notion of all mainstream Indian communities towards the Gorkhas. If we see it objectively, all the communities of the country want to use and throw the Gorkhas in India by their respective marginalization process. Might be the Gorkhas have been cursed by some one else at the time of her death. The Gorkhas are operationalized by these authors as *Sati Lay Sarap Diyako Jati* (cursed by a lady at her husband's funeral pyre in the past). The marginalization of Gorkhas are both at the level of within and outside the community itself. Within the community, poors are exploited by the rich and at the outside, the Bengalis have marginalized the entire Gorkhas including the Gorkha tea plantation workers.

At the community level, each Gorkha caste or tribe has been crazy for having the status of scheduled tribe being well polished by its communal organization.

It means each Gorkha caste or tribe does not feel secure to live in group with other fellow castes or tribes. This may be the obvious reason why we have observed that the government has been encouraging all the Gorkha castes and tribes to form their respective Gorkha caste or tribal organizations in Darjeeling hills today. If any caste is given the status of Scheduled Tribe, it becomes very happy and starts hankering after the benefits provided by the government. In this way, the entire Gorkhas have been marginalized into smaller and smaller groups of having no specific generic ethnic identity. For example, Limboo and Tamang castes of the Gorkha community are happy to get the status of Scheduled Tribe of the country very recently. In fact, they are boastful to have Scheduled Tribe status in India. They hardly realize the precarious conditions of non-tribal fellow Gorkha groups in so far as their socio-economic condition is concerned.

In this way, Gorkha castes and tribes are divided into sub-marginalized groups so as to enable others rule the entire Gorkha community accurately and easily. It indicates that now one group of Gorkha is marginalizing another group of Gorkhas. The Government of West Bengal is very happy with this development among the Gorkhas. It indicates that the external marginalization takes place latter on with the marginalization of own people by the own people. The marginalization for the people by the people and of the people and for the people is the characteristic feature of Gorkha marginalization in India in general and West Bengal in particular. First, one set of Gorkhas marginalizes another set of Gorkhas and vice-versa over the period of time and afterwards, the Bengalis comfortably marginalize the whole Gorkhas. This is in short, the history of marginalization of Gorkhas in India. Today, for example the same Gorkhas belonging to All India Gorkha League, Communist Party (Revolutionary) Marxist and Gorkha National Liberation Front and Gorkha Janamukti Party are marginalizing each other in the name of the formation of Gorkhaland in West Bengal. This marginalization by a group against another group leads to the emergence of bloodshed and other kinds of violence. Each political party among the Gorkhas takes another political party as enemy or adversary. This may be the reason why Shri Madan Tamang, the Gorkha League Leader of Darjeeling had been butchered at broad daylight at Darjeeling town that too in the most purse area.

Similarly, during the Gorkhaland Agitation under Shri Subash Ghisingh, at least eighteen hundreds to two thousands Gorkhas died fighting each other, of course, with the Sakuni Niti/Chanakya Niti of the Bengalis and Bengal Government of West Bengal through Subash Ghisingh. The formation of Gorkhaland Regional Authority by the present Gorkha Janamukti Morcha (political party) would be another glaring example of marginalization of Gorkhas in Darjeeling hills along with the tea plantation workers of North-East India. Everything has been made obscure in so far as the formation of Gorkhaland Regional Authority and the same old story of hill autonomy concept as opinioned and championed by the Communist Party (M) of India in West Bengal ever since the last three decades would take place. Where is the special achievement that most popular present Gorkha Janamukti Morcha has achieved today with the forthcoming formation of Gorkhaland Regional Authority at Darjeeling? We call in Gorkhali prover for the formation of Gorkhaland Regional Authority as *Macha Macha Macha/Bhyaguta* in the context of the political movement of Darjeeling hills ever since 1907 A.D. The rat race for limited resources articulated by Bengalis of West Bengal has been operationalized nicely among all the Gorkhas of West Bengal on the days the come tomorrow.

Another process of marginalization of Gorkhas is the luring process. All the political parties and leaders simply know how to marginalize the common Gorkhas. The luring process of the British tea planters and administrators is equally applicable today to Gorkhas at the hands of their leaders and government. In fact, it is introspected that we the Gorkhas, happen to be happy to go on procession, meeting and gathering as we enjoy with the situation even if we have to die at the spot. It may be due to the tribal character of Gorkhas. Here, the proposed Sixth Schedule approach of Shri Subash Ghisingh, the leader of Gorkha National Liberation Front appears to be true. This is what Shri Subash Ghisingh wanted to convert Darjeeling hills as tribal area in the manner of Nagaland, Mizoram, Meghalaya and Arunachal Pradesh of North-East India. If it is true, then the Sixth Schedule status of Darjeeling is much better than the forthcoming Gorkhaland Regional Authority. Ultimately, the Gorkhaland issue is boiled down to the level of regional autonomy as championed by the Communist Party (M) of India of West Bengal. Is it not the new chapter of Marginalization of Gorkhas in West Bengal?

Afno Manche/Arka Manche

The concept of *Afno Manche* (relatives) and *Arka Manche*

(unknown persons) is the responsible factor for the marginalization of Gorkhas in Darjeeling hills in particular and India in general. The person belonging to a big sort is favored and even a person who is proficient, talented and have sufficient caliber does not get support from the big sort if he is not his *Afno Manche* (Bista:1993) The *Afno Manche/Arka Manche* phenomenon has lead the Gorkhas not united. This picture is also found in the state of Sikkim. The *Afno Manche/Arka Manche* phenomenon among the Gorkhas has spoiled the whole social structure of Gorkhas in West Bengal. So, another hindrance to the ethnic unity of Gorkhas is *Afno Manche/Arka Manche* phenomenon ever since the independence of the country. A big sort Gorkha marginalizes another common Gorkha on the basis of this phenomenon. They forget the ethnicity importance when their personal interest is affected by the group interest. Simply for the name-sake of the Gorkhas, each and every Gorkha talks about the ethnic unity in West Bengal. This was reflected at the time of making Shri Prasant Tamang (Lama: 2008) as third Indian Idol from the Gorkha community of Darjeeling—a singing competition under Indian Idol programme organized by Sony Television channal in 2007.

This was rather the upsurge of emotional unity among the Gorkhas of the world that lasted long for a few days only in 2008. The sustainability of emotional unity of Gorkhas is very rare. That is why today, Shri Prasant Tamang is almost forgotten by the Gorkhas of Darjeeling-Sikkim Himalayas. The shortsighted vision of big sort Gorkhas is still another reason for their marginalization in India. So, unless and until the concept of *Afno Manche/Arka Manche* is there among the Gorkhas, there appears to be a far cry for the creation of Gorkhaland in India. This is the vision of these present authors being generated living with the Bengalis at Siliguri with our life long experience. *Kam Chalo Bahro Afal Tero Tharo*—moment, the selfishness of a person is served with the used vessel, the used vessel is thrown out to the dust bin. The same quality has been taught by the Bengalis of West Bengal to the Gorkhas in their day-to-day social relationship network. It is heard that the Gorkha leaders are being secretly threatened by the government to be jailed if they do no adhere to their terms of settlement every time from the independence of the country to today. This is possible for the Government of West Bengal as it has political power of the state. Under this threatening process, the Gorkha political leaders have to bow down their heads before the marginalization process of West Bengal Government and Bengalis of West Bengal. After that, the Gorkha leaders become very good friends of the Bengalis and West Bengal Government.

This is the entire history of Gorkha leaders right from late Shri Damber Singh Gurung to Shri Subash Ghisingh and present Shri Bimal Gurung of Gorkha Janamukti Morcha of Darjeeling. This shows that at first, the Bengal Government marginalizes with its mighty political power and dictation to the Gorkha leaders and through the Gorkha leaders, the West Bengal Government marginalizes the entire Gorkhas of West Bengal and the same policy is being followed by other states of North-East India. Aftermath of the political settlements, only the Gorkhas who are the relatives and close friends of political leaders are favored and rest of the common Gorkhas are now and again simply marginalized. This was found at the time of Shri Subash Ghisingh of Gorkha National Liberation

Front and probably the same will be there at the regime of Gorkha Janamukti Morcha in future under Shri Bimal Gurung. In the marginalization process of Gorkhas, the local Gorkha leader emerges from the old influential political party. For instance, Shri Bimal Gurung, the President of Gorkha Janamukti Morcha emerged from the Gorkha National Liberation Front of Shri Subash Ghisingh. Interestingly, all the Gorkhas at the regime of Shri Subash Ghisingh were silent instead of knowing fully that Shri Subash Ghisingh had been marginalizing the entire Gorkha community of the region for the last twenty years commencing from 1988 to 2008 in Darjeeling. Since Shri Subash Ghisingh represented the Gorkhas of Darjeeling, the Government of West Bengal also could not even dare to conduct election for the then Darjeeling Gorkha Hill Council. This is how Shri Subash Ghisingh could easily marginalize the entire Gorkahs of West Bengal in particular and India in general.

Strings for Gorkha Identity

Instead of having holistic intra-community as well as inter-community marginalization process of Gorkhas in India, they have a deep commitment towards Gorkha identity may be due to two obvious reasons, viz., homogeneity in terms of language and tribal, semi-tribal characters that are mostly loved by the Gorkhas. Secondly, increasing inter-caste and inter-tribal love marriages based on class status in the Gorkha society among the youths is still another strong thread for having strong Gorkha identity among the Gorkhas. Thirdly, *Marda Ra Parda Afnai Manche Kam Lagcha* or a Gorkha needs the support of another Gorkha only in ordeal or odd situations. Similarly, *Para Ko Deota*

Ra Nagik Ko Bhut Ma Nagik Ko Bhut Nai Kam Lagcha meaning thereby the prominent god of distant place cannot help the Gorkhas in ordeal situations while the nearest evils extend aid to the Gorkha people in such odd situations. The existence of Gorkha identity in India is always relatively under apprehension rather than comprehension among the mainstream communities. Here, in this respect, Dr. Sailen Debnath (2008), a prominent historian of North Bengal, has very lucidly stated that Bengalis of West Bengal failed to bring the Gorkhas into the mainstream life of West Bengal. Bengali thinking of being inheritors of British Raj, their penchant for promoting own community's interests at the expense of other communities is fastly marginalizing non-Bengali communities. Rather, Bengalis have succeeded to marginalize the entire Gorkhas of North Bengal right from political to socio-economic as well as cultural aspects of their life in West Bengal. The short-sighted vision of Bengalis and Government of West Bengal is responsible factor for the emergence of the concept of marginalization of Gorkhas in West Bengal. Conceptually, entire Gorkhas are humiliated, marginalized, cut into sizes rather than paste into association with West Bengal. All the Bengalis are interested just to get the things done from Gorkhas and kick them out after they got the jobs done from the Gorkhas. Having tribal or semi-tribal characters, always, the Gorkhas are put under illusion, confusion, non-transparency culture and making nowhere *(Alapatra)* in their upbringing right from 1947 to today in West Bengal. Still Gorkhas belong to jocular race.

All the Gorkha political leaders when they are embarrassed under ordeal situation created by Bengalis think nowhere except to go back to Darjeeling hills and marginalize, exploit and put under utter confusion among the fellow Gorkhas with Sakuni Niti/Chanakya Niti of Bengali political leaders who become inturn the Gurus to the Gorkha political leaders. This is also found as a bare truth if we can retrospect the history of political leaders of Darjeeling hills right from the British days to today. Even at the socio-economic-educational parlance, Gorkha like Prof. Mahendra P. Lama, the Vice-Chancellor of Sikkim University from Darjeeling, aftermath of becoming a member of National Security Council of India and being purchased by the Government of West Bengal directly or indirectly has started talking against the Gorkhaland issue which is in the sole interest of all Gorkhas of Darjeeling and India. Doing this, he is supporting Bengalis and West Bengal Government. He talks about hardware and software and stressed on software to be developed among the Gorkhas in order to compete the Bengalis in particular and Indians in general. By software, he meant to develop the Gorkha community educationally. He talks this may be due to the highhandedness of Bengalis in New Delhi as well as in Indian Parliament. But in normal life situation, he pretends to be a pure Gorkha as he is found to have been shared with common Gorkha foods, common Gorkha sentiment, common gossiping with other common Gorkhas but in reality he appeared to be crazy to be the only luminary in the Gorkha community as he intends to be invited with all jesters in important social occasions by the common Gorkhas as chief guest so that he is honored overtly by all other Gorkhas of Darjeeling-Sikkim as well as North-East Himalayas.

This is the apparent observation sprouted from his recent approach to the Gorkhaland movement in

Darjeeling hills. He is crazy for his own name, fame and honor in the Gorkha society of the region. It indicates that salabillity at others hand is the characteristic feature of Gorkha community in India. If person like Prof. Mahendra P. Lama is sold out to Bengalis then what about the common Gorkha political leaders and common Gorkhas of West Bengal and India. This is proved by his ongoing queer relationship with Gorkha Janamukti Morcha and its leader Shri Bimal Gurung. He forgets the need and importance of Gorkha identity, Gorkha sentiment, Gorkha suffering, Gorkha history and Gorkha way of life. May be because of being Economist, he is overwhelmed by materialistic world by selling his Gorkha identity to the hands of Bengalis of West Bengal and New Delhi. Still, he is Gorkha in the eyes of common Gorkhas of Darjeeling and North-East India. Like other political leaders, he is also a *Mohara* (pawn) at the hands of Bengalis of India and New Delhi. In fact, he has nothing to fight with the mighty Bengalis in India because all the Bengalis of India are against the formation of Gorkhaland in India. This was supplemented by the annoyance expressed by the entire Bengalis of the country to the Gorkhas at the time of Gorkhaland Movement under Shri Subash Ghisingh and also today under Shri Bimal Gurung of Gorkha Janamukti Morcha party of Darjeeling.

It shows that Gorkhas, no matter whether big sorts or common persons are marginalized in different fashions but the objective of marginalization is same for all the Gorkhas in India. Neither the Government of West Bengal nor the Government of India is realistic enough and truely sincere to comprehend the real problems of Gorkhas. The government is simply interested to sort out Gorkha problem politically for the time being so that at least for a few years to come by the identity problems of Gorkhas are settled or subsided. The Gorkha leaders being politically tutored by Bengali Gurus know how to make the fellow Gorkhas marginalized and earn as much money as possible within the shortest span of time. As soon a political leader becomes rich, he leaves hills sometime for Siliguri or Kolkata at the care or disposal of Bengalis and Bengal Government. But at the time of end of his regime, he takes the help of Bengal police so as to be saved himself from the possible assaults of fellow Gorkhas in hill Darjeeling. After some time at self articulated political exile at Siliguri or Kolkata, he or she returns back to hill Darjeeling to take his or her last breath at his or her birth place Darjeeling and then his or her dead body is being cremated by the fellow poor, cheated Gorkha relatives and friends who were left out of his consideration for least favor when he was on his or her heydays. These authors know all these sufferings on their thirty years of living with Bengalis at Siliguri. A Bengali is called as *Ama Diyara Bau Na Hune Jat* meaning thereby even if a Gorkha gives his mother to a Bengali on marriage, the Bengali fellow never becomes his true father. But the new Bengali father simply gives the stepfatherly treatment to the Gorkha children of the woman who is newly married to him. Lot of such examples can be found at Darjeeling hills today.

The above observation can further be supplemented by the fact that Gorkhas are really the objects of cutting into sizes by others, their simplicity as weakness but utter favor for Bengalis in India. Their stubbornness is being utilized for others' benefits and loss for their own community. Now, therefore, the days have come to tell others that Gorkhas are not merely the Bahadurs, guards and mercenary force in India but most potential human resource capital of the country. Lots of Gorkhas are educated and civilized. Most of the Bengalis think that Gorkhas are uncivilized *(asabhya)* and they (Bengalis) are highly civilized. Most of the Bengalis express doubts about the citizenship of Gorkhas and say that Gorkhas are from Nepal (meaning they are foreigners, immigrants and should not ask for any rights at par with the Bengalis), even after residing in India since last seven generations. So, Gorkhas are no more counted as sincere, committed and dedicated ethnic group in India, their very Indianness is often questioned under one pretext or the other. This is transparent from the behavioral pattern of Bengali community in relation to Gorkhas in West Bengal. Individually, a Gorkha may get some favor from a Bengali simply by selling his or her ethnic identity at the hands of the Bengali. This is apparent at the level of socio-economic, political, cultural and even educational dimensions of Gorkhas in West Bengal.

Politically, the Gorkha political leaders like Ratanlal Brahmin of Communist Party (M) of India got the opportunity of becoming a Member of Parliament through Shri Jyoti Basu, the then Chief Minister of West Bengal. Similarly, Shri R.B. Rai became the Member of Parliament as he was a Communist from Darjeeling. Prior to that Shri Damber Singh Gurung, Shri Nar Bahadur Gurung and others became the Members of Legislative Assembly of West Bengal by selling their Gorkha identity to the Congress leaders of West Bengal. They forgot their Gorkha-ness at the hands of Bengalis of West Bengal. At first, they were all having Gorkha sentiments, identity, emotions as well as true sons of the Gorkha mothers. But later on, they all were sold to the Bengalis of West Bengal. Shri Ari Bahadur Gurung (Gorkha Barrister from England) of Kalimpong got the opportunity to sign on the drafted manuscript of Indian Constitution not because of being a Gorkha but because of being the ardent follower of the then Congress Party of West Bengal and Shri B.C. Roy who had later on became the first Chief Minister of West Bengal. Although Shri Damber Singh Gurung was the leader from the Gorkha League Party of Darjeeling, yet later on, he became the Member of Legislative Assembly of West Bengal from the then Congress Party of West Bengal. All these examples show as to how the Gorkha leaders in particular and common Gorkhas of West Bengal were marginalized. In the process of marginalization, the Government of West Bengal has been successful to divide the Gorkhas of Darjeeling hills and Dooars area into manifold political colors and political parties. For instance, today there has started a rift between the Gorkha followers of Gorkha National Liberation Front and Gorkha Janamukti Morcha—both are the political parties of Gorkhas of Darjeeling. Doing this, the West Bengal Government in particular and Bengalis of West Bengal in general are very happy so that they can divide the Gorkhas into groups and used martial political power so that the political interest of West Bengal is being kept intact. Instead of having similar experience in the past, the Gorkhas are still swimming with the same Sakuni/ Chanakya Niti of West Bengal Government. The political party is of the first importance to the Gorkhas to which they always get ready to sacrifice their lives and afterwards, to the Gorkha community. This is the entire history of Gorkhas in West Bengal ever since the last one hundred years. They are the loyal dogs of West Bengal political parties leaving aside the interests of Gorkha community.

The pertinent point to note here is that instead of their division into factions, groups and segments, the Gorkhas are having their specific cultural identities, of course, they have lost their socio-economic and political identities in West Bengal. The cultural identities are carried over by their cultural manner, customs and traditions including the language. The *Dasai-Dashara* festival, *Sarau* (help in the form of cash or kind) at the time of occurring death at others houses, calling each other *Daju-Bhai* and *Didi-Bahini* are the strong cultural threads that have been the binding force among the Gorkhas of Darjeeling hills, Terai and Dooars areas of West Bengal in particular and India in general. The Nepali language is the common means of communication among the Gorkhas in India and also in West Bengal. Analysis of the Gorkha marginalization is an untold history in the country. All the communities got their respective states in India but the Gorkhas have been denied thoroughly on the ground that only the Gorkhas are immigrants or the descendents of immigrants from Nepal. Nobody talks about the Bengali immigration from Bangladesh to West Bengal in particular and India in general. Lakhs of Bangladeshi migrants have been allowed to settle in West Bengal and authorities even facilitate them by making ration cards, voter identity cards and even passports. Bengalis want to increase their numbers by settling Bangladeshis and granting them Indian citizenship which further marginalizes other non-Bengali communities. Assamese in Assam talk about Illegal Migrants, they do not want to settle Bangladeshis in their state, they want to expel them from Assam. But in West Bengal Bangladeshi immigrants are given red carpet welcome. This fact is thoroughly ignored because Bengalis have their West Bengal state to which even the Government of India scared to talk anything. As Bengalis are deeply entrenched in Central Government, they are in a position to thwart any move of the central government about the formation of Gorkhaland and thereby restore the identity status of the Gorkhas in India. This has lead to the desperation of Gorkhas in India because there is no hope to get better status in Indian society except the status of mercenary force, chowkidars, Coolies and body guards in most of the cases. We have no prejudice to individual Bengalis as in many ways Bengalis have helped us a lot to establish ourselves academically sound personalities in West Bengal. But at the community level, our status is as good as of all the Gorkhas of India.

5

The Gorkhas and Globalization

With the emergence of Globalization of Indian economy and establishment of global hut concept in India, the Gorkhas have been liberalizing themselves from the socio-economic bondage of West Bengal. Almost all the youth Gorkhas are now free to move to make their own choice as well as destiny in so far as doing any type of jobs is concerned. Almost five lakh Gorkha youths of Darjeeling and Dooars areas of West Bengal are devoting their time in India today on the jobs of their choice in various businesses and call centers. The number is increasing by leaps and bounds. The specific characteristics of youth Gorkhas are that they do their jobs as per their desire rather than due to the imposition from any corner. They appear to be very happy in working at the business call centers of the country especially in big metros like Kolkata, Bengalore, Delhi, Mumbai, Chennai etc. of the country. Of course, later on, they become the victims of Information Technology as they forget their culture, tradition and even to some extent their mother tongue, ie Nepali. At a stretch, they appear to be the global youths being dictated by the global way of life. Their health status is not so promising. So, it is apprehended that how long a youth can work in such a mechanized way of life. Most of them do not want to marry as they are satisfied with their way of life of being bachelors. It is also apprehended that they are losing whole lots of their potentialities of life and they will definitely be leading the life of weak and meek citizens of the country in future. In the light of this discussion, let us discuss about the platitude of Gorkhas in India today.

The smiling face, stubbornness, loyalty, jocular gester and commitments along with the physical smartness are the characteristic features of Gorkhas which have attracted all the communities and companies—both national and multinational to employ the Gorkhas in their business. The same thing is also found at the tea plantation frontiers of North- East India. The greatest outcome of Globalization at tea frontiers of North-East India is the informalization of tea plantation workers in the context of marginalization of Gorkhas in North-East India.

Informalization of Gorkha Tea Garden Workers

The discussion will show that how the Gorkhas have been marginalized in India. The term "informalization" involves two things, viz., self-employment and secondly, emergence of more and more female work force in tea garden sector of national economy. The tea plantation sector carries more and more the informal characters as it is an agro-based industry with the wide organizational hieararchy from the skilled managers to manual (unskilled) workers. This may be the reason why tea industry has dual characteristics viz, agriculture and industry (Xaxa: 1997). It has a manufacturing unit (factory) along with the agrarian specificities like field with tea bushes, paddy, maize, vegetables, oranges, cardamom and animal husbandry ever since its inception. The most important perceptible change taken place after the globalization is that the plantation sector has been introduced with uncertainty of works, workers and management as all of them are flying with Fight or Flight philosophy in the competitive global era. The other characteristic feature as found today in tea plantations are uncertainty of employment, avoidance of labour laws and casualisation or contractualisation of work force. The concept of decent pay with decent work as demanded by the trade unions is the point of trade union-management entanglement in West Bengal. The concept of Class as championed by Karl Marx is on the constant decay because there is no permanent work force in the tea plantations of the region. This has made the workers defenseless, free and swiming with absolute greediness for better way of living in the globalised era.

The informalization as the process of change has been accredited by the government. This has made the trade unions of Darjeeling hills ever biggest corrupted organizations of workers because the trade unions act on the absolute political unionism that cannot go against the interests of the industry and government so they have rather open options to marginalize the rank and file workers. On the other hand, no tea garden worker is directly under the grip of trade unions nor at the control of management and in this way, the control over the work force of the past has gone down forever.

The informalization of work force can thus be seen to have been proceeded on the one hand with feminization of work force to tackle the poverty and backwardness of plantation society in Darjeeling hills and Dooars and North-East India on the other. The women in the process of informalization provides a crucial link with the domestic economy and community in the process which has far reaching effects or impacts on the dynamics of plantation community of Darjeeling hills. Here, the women workers are in fact marginalized by their male counterpart.

The male counterpart hardly thinks to go on tea garden duty perfectly because the tea garden job is secondary to the males at the tea plantations. The tea industry has been brought under the purview of informalization of economy by the Government of West Bengal with its whimsical policy of tea-tourism because tourism is purely informal sector of Indian economy. Working in tea industry and working in tourism industry are directly two different pursuits of economy. Both industries at the same habitation, i.e., in tea industry appear to be a hippie philosophy. This may be the reason why this philosophy has not seen the light of the day in West Bengal till today ever since the last one decade. Secondly, the spill over effects of tea tourism is rather detrimental on the part of the plantation workers as they will be devoting their times on both the pursuits. In fact, the world famous tourist centre (Darjeeling) is polished with tea bushes as "Green Gold" ever quoted since the British days. So, tea tourism appears to be a non-reality in case of Darjeeling hills. Otherwise, the whole lot of elements of beautiful Darjeeling hills (Queen of Hills) will be finished into non-entity. Considering this, may be the half hearted efforts being taken by the Government of West Bengal and also Tea Board of India amid the emerging challenges go on to astray. This is the caution given to the government by these scholars as it is found from the opinion of the workers and also the management of Darjeeling tea industry. Sustaining tea industry in the Himalayan niche is simply an act of image making drama of the government for the interest of West Bengal. Otherwise, the Darjeeling Himalayan Railway, the recipient of world heritage status will loose its potency. The charmness that the tourists accord through their journey from Siliguri to Darjeeling on the Darjeeling Himalayan Railway will end if tea industry- the green gold zone is dwindled for ever. So, in fact, it is the national challenge for government not to end the tea industry in Darjeeling Himalayas. If tea industry is closed down like Dooars areas of West Bengal then it will be followed by the end of tourism industry for ever in Darjeeling because the snow tops of the great Kanchenjunga Mountain will deplete forever and thereby the beauty of Darjeeling will further decline.

This is a kind of informalization effect of globalization for sustaining tea industry by the Government of West Bengal in Darjeeling and not for the sake of development of Gorkha people thereof alone. So, tourism industry and tea industry are two different pursuits of national economy which should not be mixed together to create a new blend of taste for the people concerned. These two industries have their individual organisational objectives which can in no way be blended together.

Globalization and Productivity of Gorkha Tea Garden Workers

The process of informalization of tea industry is being directly interlinked with productivity level of the workers instead of the fact that productivity is a holistic concept. Every management of tea industry claims that labour productivity is only the yardstick to measure the prosperity of tea industry in the globalized era. Let us discuss the various facets of the productivity of tea industry in the globalized era. In fact, globalization opts for better productivity every day. The very blemishness that has been labeled against the Indian tea industry is due to the low level of tea garden productivity ever since 1991. The productivity of the agro-based industry like tea is the composite whole of very many factors of production involved in the tea industry as the tangible factors of production (Bhowmik:2008). In fact, productivity is also considered as the balance between the way of thinking and doing things in the industry. Tea industry is to be considered as a corporate whole having the ownership of both the management and workers. In this context, it is seen that tea industry has been solely made the property of owners and management and not the workers who are rather kept at the periphery in so far as owning the industry in concerned. So, let us discuss the different factors of productivity. The issue 'productivity' has coined the day in the era of globalization under the competitive market economy. It means that the market is only the determining variable of production. Of course, this is directly affecting the working class of the country as a whole. It is more effective to tea industry as it is basically a labour intensive industry of the country. Today, interestingly, the issue "productivity" has been addressed to the productivity of the workers. However, the other factors of production also need to be properly addressed. But the major question is whether really the productivity of labour is a must today to compete the world market or not. The common perception in tea industry is that production can be increased only through the higher labour productivity which is absolutely wrong. However, productivity can be improved if other material factors of production are also improved. The argument stated by the tea garden management that improvement in labour productivity can only improve the overall productivity of tea industry is false as Gorkha tea plantation workers being the prototype of Gorkha community need no such explanation as they were labourours in the past and also at the present juncture and this is the main reason why the entire Gorkhas called as the *Kati Khane Jati* (labourous community) in the world. Therefore, rather other factors need improvement that include expansion of the area under tea cultivation in existing 95 thousand hectares of vacant land of tea gardens of Darjeeling hills (Nag: 2008), improvement in the age of tea bushes and replanting of ageing tea bushes. Let us explain the whole story.

As it has been an accepted fact that the age of tea bush is an important factor for tea garden productivity. Normally, the tea bush achieved its prime potency in terms of output of green tea leaves from the age of five to thirty years. Almost fifty percept of tea bushes in Darjeeling hills are over fifty years of age resulting which the potency level has already been decreased. In this respect, hardly much importance is given to replant new tea bushes by uprooting old tea bushes by the tea companies. Thus, merely improving the labour productivity can not suffice the purpose for overall increase in productivity level of tea gardens in Darjeeling hills.

Another factor for increasing productivity is the yield per hectare. In Darjeeling, the productivity per hectare is hardly 566 kilograms of made tea per year. Inspite of having almost two hundred years of history of the Darjeeling tea industry, yield per hectare could not be increased by the companies.

Still another problem for not increasing the productivity of tea in Darjeeling hills is due to the fact that Darjeeling tea is purely orthodox which fetches highest price in international market. But the profit earned from the market is hardly utilized for the expansion of the industry. Forget about the human side of development. The so-called social clause paradigm of globalization has been thrown at the dust bin (Chitra: 2009).

Very recently, the negligence of tea garden workers and thereby resulting in decreasing labour productivity is noticed by the concerned people due to the following reasons:-

1. The tea plantation workers have been experienced with queer nature and low propensity of tea garden owners and management over the last few decades that they always hanker after prompt profits without replanting new tea bushes and also they do not want to wait for gestation period of new tea clones that are being planted for future production. It proved that they are not really industrialists but traders. This has really

frustrated the workers to see for alternate jobs and engagements giving secondary importance to tea garden jobs. It was found at Bernesbeg tea estate and North Tukvar tea estate of Darjeeling hills that most of the male youngsters as workers are found busy even in high plucking seasons carrying the alcohols from Jorethang town of Sikkim which is located at just the opposite side of these tea plantations of Darjeeling hills. The hundreds of male workers are absent in the garden jobs for months together especially during the agrarian harvesting and sowing seasons of the year.

2. The work culture of tea plantations in Darjeeling hills has been disturbed due to the political agitations in the region. Nobody bothers about the work which has resulted into the increase of absenteeism among the *Hazira* (permanent) workers. The percentage of absenteeism goes up to 50.0% in high plucking season. This enforces the management to use *Thicka* (temporary) workers. It is found that due to the use of *Thicka* workers, in many gardens, the tea bushes have been spoiled due to over coarse pluckings. This has been found to have affected the productivity of tea bushes in next round of plucking.

3. The workers feel that the tea gardens are simply the place to restore their identity by keeping their houses in tact by maintaining the same in regular interval because the management has left the idea of repairing the tea garden labour quarters. Forget about the construction of new

labour quarters for the workers in Darjeeling hills. The local political parties also ask the workers to make households theirs as per the agenda of their Himalayan trade unions ever since the last three decades. The ethnicity issue predominate the industrialization process in the region. Whose industrialization—of West Bengal or of Darjeeling hills—the workers asked this question when we were conducting the field work in Darjeeling tea gardens.

4. It is found that tea garden management wants to earn as much as possible within short span of time without having long term vision for the upliftment of people and industry. A popular slogan is gaining the ground today in Darjeeling as "SHORT CUT MAKES LIFE WEALTHY, HEALTHY AND WANT NOT". This short cut method in every aspect of tea garden life appears to be a new industrial philosophy mostly at first propounded by the management and then labour and still latter on followed by all concerned. The owners are busy to invest the profit earned from Darjeeling tea industry elsewhere rather than on tea industry of the region. It indicates that every body is in the same boat. This may be due to the uncertainty of tea industry in the country in general and Darjeeling hills in particular in the era of globalization.

5. In fact, productivity is nobody's headache in Darjeeling tea industry today. The major political parties of West Bengal are busy with their respective political gains and hardly have constructive visions on Darjeeling tea industry.

In this respect, the Government of West Bengal has also very casual outlook to Darjeeling tea industry more particularly the workers. Simply the West Bengal government is interested with handsome revenue to be accrued from Darjeeling tea industry which gives almost 900 crores per year.

6. WHO BELLS THE CAT is the overall approach of the government both at the level of local administration and the state administration in so far as the improvement of productivity is concerned that leads to the improvement in the quality aspect of Darjeeling orthodox tea in the global market in the era of globalization.

7. Finally, the tea garden workers do not care much about the industry as they by now and then are able to understand the limited role of industry for heir socio-economic upliftment. The very difference between the upliftment and development is totally known to the workers over the period of last six decades of independence. All the workers stated that nobody can really do miracle for their development. Their commitment to the industry is not at all counted upon by the companies and management and one government comes and goes after fulfilling its interest in the region. They said that *Bhira Bata Lare Pani Kilo Ritay, Bhag Lae Khai Pani Kilo Ritay* meaning thereby whether the cow is fallen from the hill top or eaten by the jungle tiger is same. Even if the tea industry is closed down, it matters less to them. By workers, they know that they are born for workers and died as workers only because

Darjeeling tea industry. The informalization has been further strengthening by the introduction of Panchayati Raj system in tea plantations of the region. The National Rural Employment Guarantee Act, 2005 of Govt of India has been affecting the tea garden productivity as many youths among the workers do better prefer the jobs of NERGA scheme as they get Rs. 138/- per head per day. So, they give secondary importance to tea garden jobs as they simply get Rs. 67/- per day per head. The potential tea garden work force has been shifting their loyalty to NEGRA works. The experience shows that the permanent work force as potential work force is leaving the tea garden jobs which do not provide two square meals to their families. This has lead to the end of concept of working class of tea industry because the workers who are working outside the tea gardens are earning good money and changing their class affiliation. So, labour as a distinct class by itself has been vanishing from the soil of tea plantations of the region. *Garib Guruba* (a poor stock) of today becomes *Hunai Khane Manche* (rich stock) tomorrow in Darjeeling.

The old Master-Servant relationship at the tea industry has changed into Neo-Master Servant relationship because no worker can be hired and fired today rather workers are to be pleased in order to get the works get done by the management. This may be the reason why today management addresses the workers with *Daju-Bhai* (brothers) or *Didi-Bahini* (sisters) and with other rich cultural jesters instead of calling the workers as *Kamanee Coolies* as in the past with all derogatory terminologies. Of course, this scenario is found today due to the political agitations in the region. Locally, at least, the management can not misbehave the workers in the earlier fashion. But compared to earlier days, the potentialities of tea garden workers can not be harnessed properly. In fact, no worker believes the management. Simply to supplement their income, mostly female workers do the tea garden jobs. In the agitation period, management has to simply do that which the local political party in power wants to do in regard to the modus operandi of the plantations. The tea industry management and Government of West Bengal do the same while dealing with the potential work force of Darjeeling hills. Both have followed the same type of technique and philosophy over the period of last sixty two years of independence of the country. It shows that globalization as an influencing force has made the termination of potential work force of tea industry of the region.

Structural Adjustment Under the Globalization

The structural adjustment policy under the Globalization has left the impression at the tea gardens that permanent workers are to be decreased by utilizing the temporary work force. Almost 97.0% of the workers at high plucking season in tea plantations of Darjeeling are temporary workers who are in fact the casual and contractual workers. Such structural adjustment policy has of course, benefited the tea industry temporarily but in the long run it will affect the industry adversely. The structural adjustment policy has not been applied in other aspects of tea industry. This may be the apparent reason why many tea gardens have been closed down for ever in West Bengal. The lavish way of life of the management has not been adjusted stating that they have tough life at the plantations followed by their higher quality of life to be maintained at the plantations. They have to be adjusted themselves in such a way that they can not mix up with the rank and file workers freely at the plantations. The structural adjustment policy also left the impression that they are as good as British planters who have to follow the British legacy. Later on in their life, it become very difficult for the managers to adjust with the common Gorkha way of life in the Gorkha society and this may be the reason why many ex-managers pursue social welfare activities just to adjust themselves with the society and have safe identity at the society.

Otherwise, they are looked down upon by the common people of Gorkha community. The Gorkha concept of *Marda Ra Parda Afnai Manche Kam Lagcha* meaning thereby in ordeal situations, own men come to rescue them is applicable to all Gorkhas no matter whether they are managers or common workers. This may be the reason why many good managers left the post of tea garden managers and have opted to work as the tea consultants and advisors. For example, Shri J.P. Gurung, Mr. Harish Mukhia, Mr. Prem Kumar Tamang etc.—the renowned managers of Darjeeling tea industry left the post of managers and they are working as tea consultants and advisors today. Many managers rather preferred to involve in tea trade and also work as tea brokers. It indicates the fact that sociology of the structural adjustment policy has mostly affected the tea garden management rather than the rank and file workers. No more, the old proverb *Chia Ko Bhot Ma Paisa Falcha* meaning thereby tea bushes fetch easy money has dominated the day in Darjeeling.

Earlier, the Gorkhas were considered as *Khati Khane*

Jat (laborous community) who used to fully devote at tea plantation jobs but now they are interested in other sectors of economy of both the national and international organizations. Thus, in so far as the structural adjustment policy of globalization is concerned, the Gorkhas have proved that once they were loyal British mercenary force and then the loyal British tea garden Coolies and now the loyal Global service sector workers. So, the structural adjustment policy of economy has made the Gorkhas transformed themselves in other way round in their socio-economic pursuits in the entire world. Where there are Gorkhas, they are meant for hard working people. This is proved by the fact that hardly we get Gorkha beggars in the countryside especially outside Darjeeling hills. This shows that they are born for hard work and hard work only across the world. Their sincerity has enabled them to adjust themselves with any kind of job, any place and any people as well as any community of the world.

Kaman and *Kamanees*

Literally, by *Kaman,* we understand backward location and the workers who are staying in the backward location are called *Kamanees*. By backwardness, two approaches had been clearly operationalized in the history of the Himalayan tea industry, viz, backwardness due to their isolation and secondly, backwardness due to the ignorance of the people of the plantations (Sharma: 2009). The backwardness could well be sustained till the outburst of Gorkhaland agitation in Darjeeling tea plantations between 1984-1988 when lakhs of people from the Gorkha community of Darjeeling hills started coming down to Siliguri and thereby they could experience the sorrows of living with Bengalis as marginalized human stock. Another meaning of *Kaman* means the area under the command of an English manager. The entire area used to come under his command where even the British Government could not intervene without the compliance of the manager or planter of the plantation. Creation of *Kamans* was exclusively the British effort to establish the region isolated from rest of the country. Making *Kaman* isolated means to marginalize the plantation zone of Darjeeling hills. The tea garden areas along with the workers were therefore made isolated and thereby marginalized. The *Kamanees* were considered as brutal British labour force in Darjeeling hills. Every person living in urban area used to have a kind of fear psychosis of the *Kamanees* who in one way or other were considered as butchers or men hunters if they became angry. They hardly used to hesitate to chop up the heads of human beings. In the process, even many managers were killed in Darjeeling tea gardens.

The recent instance is the assassination of manager of Rungmook and Cedar tea estate of Darjeeling during the early eighties of last century (Labor: 1989). This has left impression for the civilized and educated Gorkhas of Darjeeling that the *Kamanees* are savage people who hardly hesitate to fight with others till death. This has made the Gorkha plantation workers excluded and therefore exclusively marginalized. This might be the reason why at the time of Gorkhaland agitation of Shri Subash Ghisingh, the managers of tea plantations used to have bodyguards with weapons including the explosive ones. Therefore, at the micro level, the Gorkha tea plantation workers are marginalized by their own urban community dwellers of Darjeeling hills.

The above discussion makes it clear that the marginalization is not merely a macro phenomenon but it may be of both micro and macro phenomenon. At microscopic level, the Gorkha tea plantation workers are marginalized by their own community of the urban areas and *Thulo Manchees* and at the macroscopic level, the workers are apparently marginalized by the management/owners of the plantations as well as the Government of West Bengal in very many ways. It shows that the proneness to marginalization is abundant among the Gorkha tea plantation workers in particular and Gorkhas in general in India.

The Little Alms for Gorkha Satiation

Providing little alms in the name of welfare facilities as per the provision of Plantation Labour Act, 1951 has become customary for the tea planters just to justify their stand to the government and people at large. The cut on social cost of production appears to be the Guru mantra for management so as to consider the cost cut of production on labour front of the plantations. In fact, nobody knows the quality aspect of cost involved for the welfare aspects of the workers. The type of ration provided to the workers is no less quality of the food stuff given to the cattles. Similarly, the hospital facility is simply ritualistic ones. Whatever the expenses come under medical treatment at nursing homes and hospitals outside the region at Siliguri or Kolkata are not reimbursed by the management but by the workers themselves from their own wallet. The management and owners thought that giving little alms in the form of welfare incentives makes the Gorkha tea plantation workers happy and satiated. In this way, the Gorkha tea plantation workers are from the welfare point of view exclusively marginalized. Here, if any influential trade union leader raises any objection, then he will be again purchased by the management/owners with handsome ransom.

This proneness of Gorkhas to be purchased by others has obsessed the entire history of Gorkha living in Darjeeling hills and tea plantation trade union leaders of the region are also in the same track. The poverty of sufficiency or abundance is the characteristic feature of Gorkha community in so far as their socio-economic life in the country is concerned. Every time, the Gorkha political leaders, the Gorkha trade union leaders and obviously Gorkhas as a whole are being purchased by Bengalis in West Bengal and other communities of the country.

Every political leader from Gorkha community tries to purchase the other common Gorkhas of the region with little alms and left leadership of the Gorkhas and Gorkha workers as soon as his interest is fulfilled. Hardly the leaders including the trade union leaders speak the whole story of the realities to the workers about every thing including the result of collective industrial level bargaining and political dialogues held in Kolkata or New Delhi. This is the spectacular feature of tea garden industrial level agreements ever since the time of the independence of the country. This is due to the absence of rank and file worker trade union leaders who attend the industrial level agreements either at Siliguri or Kolkata of West Bengal as the true representatives of the tea garden workers.

Gorkha Expectations from West Bengal Government

Step-motherly treatment of West Bengal Government to Gorkhas of Darjeeling-Dooars areas of West Bengal is responsible factor for the backwardness of the areas ever since the independence of the country. Simply making the region and people under neo-colonialism is the characteristic feature of the Government of West Bengal. The West Bengal Government knows how to do hypocrisy over other minor communities of the state. This might be the reason why every other community people hates the Bengali community by the core of their hearts as Bengalis consider the people of other communities as backward, idiots and uncivilized. These are the characteristics ever put up by the Bengalis to the Gorkhas of West Bengal.

Since the Gorkhas do not have sufficient number of Members of Parliament as well as Members of Legislative Assembly in West Bengal, the one or two MLAs or MPs from Darjeeling hills can not make any significant propoganda in the state legislature and Indian Parliament in favor of the Gorkhas of India. Thus, the expectation of Gorkhas from the Government of West Bengal and Government of India is almost negligible. Rather other communities of the country can do something for the Gorkhas but not the Bengalis of West Bengal unless it is in favor of Bengalis of West Bengal. The Gorkhas are therefore in a mess in so far as the marginalization process of Bengalis is concerned in the state of West Bengal. This is experienced by us being Gorkhas of West Bengal. This may be the reason why youngsters Gorkhas of West Bengal do not have any future in West Bengal and this may be the apparent reason why most of the

Gorkha youngsters are on comple mobility across the country and even abroad today in search of their life long destiny.

Globalization and Gorkha Society

As we have already mentioned the fact in our previous books that Globalization and Gorkha society since time immemorial have synchronized together as every Gorkha tries to go out in some unknown place to do something noble for better livelihood. We being the simple Gorkhas from Kalimpong sub-division of the district of Darjeeling, West Bengal, came to Siliguri in early eighties and made ourselves saleable in the market in so far as our educational and professional endeavors were concerned. In the process, we had to adjust ourselves with the vagaries of the situation with Bengalis as well as some fellow Gorkhas at Siliguri. Every Gorkha believes that nobody can help him unless he helps himself.

The Gorkha community has a very rich cultural touch regarding the mobility of the Gorkhas as we have the rich saying as *"Chora Ko Jat Ki Ran Ma Ki Ban Ma"* meaning thereby the son of a Gorkha should either die in war fighting with enemy or in jungle fighting with wild animals. This is similar as per the ethos of Globalization today. It indicates that although the Gorkhas are the Himalayan highlanders but they have to make fortunes at difficult places of work across the world. If it is so, then we can generalize that Gorkhas and Globalization are two sides of the same coin. Service to others as depicted by the Globalization is very much found with the blood and sweats of Gorkhas. The Gorkhas died for others' fortunes while the people like Bengalis die for their own fortunes only. This is the basic difference between Gorkhas and Bengalis in India. We, the authors are the living examples of this statement. We did lot for the sectional interest of Bengalis but finally we were made nowhere in order to do something better for our personal interests. However, the Globalization enables the Gorkhas to explore the best possible means for their constant betterment. The Globalization helps the Gorkhas to go to any parts of the world for better work and living. This might be the reason why today in every country we found the Gorkhas working nicely and acceptable to all global communities. In U.S.A., U.K., Australia, Germany, France, Italy, Arabian countries, Africa etc., the Gorkhas are very popular. Only for Bengalis, Gorkhas are the subject of their ethnically hatred human stock because they are demanding Gorkhaland in their more than five centuries habitated land.

They made the Darjeeling, Dooars, Terai and North Eastern hill terrains habitable on which the communities like Bengali, Assamese and other tribals have started putting their carnal eyes giving ethnocentric sentiments. For instance, historically, North Bengal had never been incorporated on the political map of Bengal prior to the annexation of the area under the British Raj. This is indicated by the nomenclature of the places of the region. For example, Siliguri which means in Gorkha term as the fort of stones, Jalpaiguri—A Fort surrounded by water, Dhupguri—the fort of scented sticks, Raja Bhatkhawa—the place where a Gorkha king had taken his meal, Mallaguri—the fort of Malla kings of Nepal. Even the land up to the River Brahmaputra of Assam, Bhutan and Sikkim were once upon a time under the sovereignty of the House of Gorkhas of Nepal. Why these facts have been hidden by the so-called intellectual Bengali historians? It means that the history ever written by the Bengali Historians are completely biased.

Socio-culturally, the Gorkha culture has deep roots in these areas although now the Bengalis are trying to convert forcefully these areas under the process of Bengali ethnocentrism. We do not understand why knowing fully these facts, the so-called Bengali intellectuals are blind to state the bare historical truth. Of course, Bengalis know how to make good people of other communities their's but evicting the common people of other communities diplomatically or with full of Sakuni/Chanakya Niti as well as mighty political power of the state of West Bengal and this is their nature and culture. Every step of the Bengalis in every aspect of their life reflects their distinct vested interests by undermining the interests of other communities.

Globalization and Market Economy

Globalization stresses for the open market economy in which the Gorkhas are most suited customers as they are appeared to be the prospective customers of goods and services provided by the open market economy. The Gorkhas are very descent customers to all businessmen at Siliguri who hardly ill-bargain and thereby every shop keeper of Siliguri becomes very happy if a Gorkha comes to his shop to purchase anything on his shop while the Bengali shop keeper becomes quite unhappy if another Bengali comes to his shop as Bengalis make ill-bargainings. This is transparent from the Siliguri market situation. So, Globalization and market economy are very much attuned to the Gorkha culture and way of life. In fact, the Gorkhas are mostly major customer community at the Siliguri market. This may be the reason why if Darjeeling-Dooars where all people are Gorkhas are under strike and deadlock, then there will be at least a loss of seven to nine crores of ruppes in a day at the Siliguri mega market as it has been declared by the Chamber of Commerce and Industry, Siliguri. Thus, the market economy ethos of globalization and Gorkha community are complimentary to each other. The instant picture of Globalization can be seen at Darjeeling town itself where every foreigner says that Darjeeling appears to be a foreign country and in no way it does appeared to be the part and parcel of Indian West Bengal.

The Gorkhas Cut into Sizes

Bengalis are by heart interested to cut the Gorkhas into their sizes so as to fulfill their vested interests. The similar constitutional rights being exercised by the Bengalis are denied to the Gorkhas in West Bengal. This is apparent from the politics for organizing meeting at Darjeeling by Communist Party (M) of India of West Bengal which has already allowed by the Bengal Government while the same right of organizing similar meeting at Siliguri is denied to Gorkha Janamukti Morcha as well as Communist Revolutionary (M) Party of Darjeeling hills today by the Government of West Bengal. This supplements the parochial as well as communal approach of Bengalis of West Bengal. This is nothing except to cut the Gorkhas into sizes on the political front. Such a cut into sizes technique of West Bengal Government is being extended to each and every aspect of socio-economic, political, educational and even cultural life of Gorkhas in West Bengal but the globalization says such things are to be avoided promptly. Even if some favors are given to some Gorkhas in West Bengal but they are all relative to the Bengali vested interests and nothing else at their isolation.

6

An Academic Conclusion

THE UNBIASED ACADEMIC RESEARCH AND ANALYSIS ON GORKHAS OF INDIA IS THE ULTIMATE NEED OF THE HOUR IN ORDER TO GIVE PROPER GUIDANCE TO THE SCHOLARS OF THE FUTURE OF OUR COUNTRY SO THAT THE ENTIRE GORKHAS ARE BROUGHT INTO THE MAINSTREAM OF NATIONAL LIFE OF THE COUNTRY. The Gorkhas had every hunch to be proud of being called Indians but not as the integral part of West Bengal. The Gorkhas wish that Bengalis should not endeavor to make the Gorkhas their slaves, confiscate the land of Gorkhas which had never been the part and parcel of West Bengal historically and finally do not intterrupt on the propagation of Gorkha culture in the region as per the Bengali fashion.

The marginalization process of Gorkhas from all corners of their life by denying their right to Self-Determination has to be ended now and now only in order to really establish the fact that Bengalis are the proponents of termination of ethnic exploitation in the world. The instances shown in the book is examplary and not exchaustic ones and therefore it is a subject for further empirical research in an objective manner. The whole history, geography, society and culture of Indian Gorkhas are to be studied at length and rewrite in a de novo way.

Socio-Economic Determinants

Socio-economic determinants of the Gorkhas should be studied by the scholars from within the community of Gorkhas. No reliance is therefore to be made on the writings of Bengalis as they are wholeheartedly biased in so far as the Gorkhas of India is concerned. This is our observation on the basis of our last thirty years of research experience gathered while living with Bengalis of West Bengal. How the Bengalis can understand the culture, blood, sweats, language, sentiments, emotions and very way of looking things by the Gorkhas. The socio-economic determinants of Gorkhas can in no way be comprehensible by the black speckles of other communities including Bengali community of the country. The socio-economic determinants are rather the inbuilt mechanisms of the Gorkhas who can better understand the determinants rather than other communities. How a Bengali does understand the Gorkha problems, their sentiments, emotions, feelings and expectation of their lives?

Bengali Sense of Cultural Superiority and Overlordship

Bengalis in general and Bengali *bhadraloks* in particular have a mindset which leads them to think that the British have bequeathed them the state of West Bengal to govern in their place and other communities like

Hindi-speaking people, tribals like Santhals, Mundas, Oraons, and Gorkhas of Darjeeling hills are subject race. The jobs, education, seats in legislature and other amenities are meant only for Bengalis, and rest are left out to rot where they are. After partition more than 70 per cent of Bengal gone out to become East Pakistan and later Bangladesh, the present state of West Bengal later incorporated many territories which were never part of Bengal historically, but the Bengali mindset refuses to accept this loss and thinks the new areas merged into state as real Bengal. Bengalis living in West Bengal do not want to understand that real Bengal is gone, and what is in their hands is a shadow *(chhaya)* of original Bengal. They even fail to take into account that the present day West Bengal is inhabited by other non-Bengali speaking population who are living here since many generations and they are as original settlers as the Bengali themselves. Bengali mindset is of exclusive nature like German mindset during Hitler's rule. Their sense of linguistic, racial and cultural superiority is somewhat akin to German's during Hitler's rule. They do not think equal of other non-Bengali people in the state, even if the Constitution of India guarantees equal status to all its citizens. This stagnant parochial thinking is alienating not only Gorkhas but also other non-Bengali people as well. There is no effort of inclusive administration or providing inclusive opportunity to non-Bengali population. Bengali political leadership took part in freedom movement, and gained an undue advantage in Indian politics in subsequent decades. One can not imagine an Indian Government without a Bengali minister with a heavyweight portfolio. Their clout is immense and they snub any and every effort by demanding equal opportunity or equal treatment at the earliest. So an effort should be made by academicians to study the alienation of non-Bengali communities in West Bengal and the sense of *ati-sabhya* (highly civilized i.e. Bengalis) and *asabhya* (uncivilized or less civilized, i.e. non-Bengalis) among Bengalis. One can snatch any/all property from a Bengali, but one can not snatch his sense of cultural superiority however poor he might be. For illegal migrants from Bangladesh, Bengali officials will make ration cards, voter identity cards, and passports for them without much inquiry or much delay. In case of other non-Bengali communities, living in West Bengal since generations they will be asked *baccha kahan paida kiya, muluk me, iska ration card nahi banega*. The non-Bengali people are told to come another day, the form is not filled correctly, or simply they are made to move from pillar to post for anything getting done from any government department. Things get easier if anyone becomes supporter of ruling party, works for the party, and takes part in organizing meetings, rally, pasting posters, writing slogans on walls, or even taking part in violent activities on behalf of the ruling party of West Bengal. The step-motherly treatment and humiliations meted out everyday has created a deep schism in the social fabric of West Bengal. The academicians or intellectuals of West Bengal should also look into these facts.

The Gorkhas at the Crossroad

The West Bengal Government should leave the dialogue of stating that hill Darjeeling is to be developed. If the government was really interested to develop

Darjeeling, what it was doing for the last six decades of independence. It is simply a hippie philosophy to say so today when the region has become politically volatile or hot pot. In fact, the West Bengal Government is interested merely to develop Siliguri and Kolkata. Nobody believes that it will develop hill Darjeeling. The Kolkata centric and Siliguri centric development process of West Bengal Government is responsible factor for the emergence of various ethnic agitations in North Bengal. The Adivasis of Dooars (Jalpaiguri), Koches of Coochbehar and Terai areas of Darjeeling are also completely not happy living with the Bengalis of West Bengal. The Gorkhas are now on the crossroad in the sense that either they should die hard for realisation of the Gorkha identity or they should constantly struggle with the Bengalis of West Bengal by motivating the Government of India and thefore the Government of India also should see the genuineness of the socio-economic, cultural, educational as well as political problems of Indian Gorkhas.

The Way Ahead for the Gorkhas

The road ahead for the Gorkhas is very tough and challenging because all the Bengalis of West Bengal are on the defensive side in so far as sustaining the region and Gorkha people colonial is concerned. Colonising the Gorkhas is the characteristic feature of West Bengal people and Government. Marginalisation and colonizing Darjeeling Hills is the one point programmme of the Government of West Bengal and Bengalis of West Bengal. It is very easy to talk about the liberalization of Gorkhas politically but it appears to be a tough job to make them really liberalized from the age old system of colonialism of West Bengal. The fruit of colony is very dear and lovable to Bengalis but not the people who are being apparently colonized. Who wants to leave golden Darjeeling to Gorkhas instead of keeping by Bengalis of the state of West Bengal permanently? In casual manner, the present day Bengalis state that Darjeeling is no more so beautiful as it was in the past, not as natural as it was in the past. Darjeeling is clumsy and unhygienic place but our point is this that if these are the established malaises of Darjeeling, then why the West Bengal Bengalis have kept Darjeeling under the political map of West Bengal? Why not the West Bengal Government has been liberalizing Darjeeling and Darjeeling Gorkhas from its colonial rule and therefore it can be an obvious queery for all concerned intellectuals except the Bengali intellectuals. It shows that the West Bengal is as good as British colonizer for Darjeeling and it is a matter of bare fact that a colonizer can never become the exponent of democracy in the world. So, the Gorkhas have to strongly fight for the restoration of democracy at Darjeeling. There is no democracy at Darjeeling since the last one decade, no democratic election to the public bodies have been held, when, as per the democratic norm, there should have been election to be held at every five years to the public bodies.

End of Ethnocentrism

The government ethnocentrism of West Bengal is responsible factor for the emergence of various political agitations in west Bengal. So, West Bengal Bengalis must leave the habit of being the followers of ethnocentrism in the process of development. Otherwise, the Singur story will now and then repeat in every nook and corner of West Bengal. The ethnocentrism is directly against the ethos of Globalization because Globalization calls for global culture, global economy, global human resource stocks and globalism as a way of life. Whereever there is a rule of ethnocentrism there is no democracy, there is no globalism and there is no global culture. In order to be free from ethnocentrism, Bengalis must see other communities at par with themselves. Making everything their's by undermining others' interests is the greatest curse of their socio-economic and political life in West Bengal which had brought and will be brought constant challenges to the Bengalis of West Bengal and the Government of West Bengal.

Why Gorkhas are Denied of Their Ethnic Identity in India?—A Concluding Remark

The Bengalis scared of Gorkhas due to the history of Gorkhas expansionist philosophy that was restored by the House of Gorkhas of Nepal in early 18th century. But the point is that now the Indian Gorkhas are completely merged with the national way of life by serving in Indian Gorkha Regiment, other forces, offices and all walks of life of Indian sub-continent. They do not have the sense of ethnocentrism whenever they pursue anything in the country. Instead of serving the country for the last five centuries, they are denied of their existence and identity. Rather Gorkhas are better patriots of the nation, better soldiers of the nation, committed work force of the country and committed populace of the country.

There is no doubt about their sincerity, devotion, commitment and contribution to the nation building process of the country. If it is so, where is the harm of giving separate identity to the Gorkhas of the country since their language (Nepali) has been given constitutional recognition by the country. If their language is one of the Indian languages, then where is the harm to accord their separate identity at the Constitution of country through the formation of Gorkhaland in India? The Indian Gorkhas of 17th century and Indian Gorkhas of 21st century are totally different as they do not have any commitment to the country like Nepal, no association with Nepal and no affiliation to the Nepalese Government of Nepal. The final point is to add that if the Nepali language is recognised in India as one of the Indian languages then how the speakers of this language are foreigners, as alleged by Bengalis time to time in West Bengal. One more point is that if the persons of Indian origin who are successful in countries like Fiji, Mauritius, Surinam, Guyana, Trinidad and Tobago, etc. can become presidents andprime ministers there and accepted as such worldwide, then why not any person of Nepalese origin or Gurkha in India can be found suitable for occupying higher posts in India. Gorkhas as naturalised citizens of India should be considered suitable for all posts and there should not be any discrimination in their appointments to higher posts. Other mainstream Indian community should also change their attitude towards the Gorkhas and think one of their own among many Indian communities.

References

Socio-Economic Life of Ciinchona Plantation Workers India, N.L. Publishers, Dibrugarh (Assam), 1997 by Dr. Khemraj Sharma.

Tea Industry in India: An Introduction, N.L. Publishers, Dibrugargh (Assam), 1999, by Dr. Khemraj Sharma

Himalayan Tea Plantation Workers, N.L. Publishers, Siliguri, 2000, by Dr. Khemraj Sharma.

Sociology of Indian Tea Industry, Mittal Publications, New Delhi, 2005 by Dr. Khemrj Sharma.

Tea Plantation Workers in a Himalayan Region, Mittal Publications, New Delhi, 2003.

Agony of Plantation Workers in North-East India, Kalpaz Publications, New Delhi, 2008 by Dr. Khemraj Sharma and Shri Tapan Chandra Das.

Globalization and Plantation Workers in North-East India, Kalpaz Publications, New Delhi, 2009, by Dr. Khemraj Sharma and Shri Tapan Chandra Das.

Plantation Sociology of North-East India, Abhijeet Publications, New Delhi, 2010 by Dr. Khemraj Sharma

*Darjeeling-Dooars People and Place under Bengal's Neo-Colonial Rule,*Bikas Jana Sahitya Kendra, Darjeeling, 2008 (in 2 Vols.) by D.S. Bomjan.

Gorkha Conquests: Causes and Consequences of Unification of Nepal with particular reference to Eastern Nepal, 1991, Oxford University Press, Calcutta, by Dr. Kumar Pradhan.

Globalization and Industrial Relations in Tea Plantations, Abhijeet Publications, Delhi, 2010 by Debabrata Mitra.

West Bengal in Doldrums, N.L.Publishers, Siliguri, 2008 by Dr. Sailen Debnath.

Social and Political Tensions in North Bengal (Since 1947), N.L. Publishers, Siliguri, by Dr. Sailen Debnath.

The History of Indian Tea Industry, Weidenfel and Nicholson, London, 1967 by Perceival Griffith

Jefrey James Oar Jonston, A. D. Printers, Siliguri, 1989 by Jiwan Labar.

The Role of Tea Planters in Creating the Demand of Separate Gorkhaland in Sailen Debnath (Ed.) *Social and Political Tensions in North Bengal* (Since 1947), 2007 by Soumen Nag.

The Gorkhas: Their Manners, Customs and Country, Cosmo Publications, New Delhi, 1976, by W.B. Northey and C.J. Morris.

Bengal District Gazetteers "Darjeeling", Logos Press, New Delhi, 1947, L.S.S.O'Malley.

Socio-Economic and Political Problems of Tea garden Workers, Mittal Publications, 2006, New Delhi, by S.N. Singh, Amarendra Narain and Purenendu

Kumar.

Issues and Challenges of Labour under Globalization, 2008, Abhijeet Publications, New Delhi, by G. Panneerselvam.

Gorkha Haruka Rithividi Raa Sanskriti (In Nepali), 2000, Ajako Sahitya Prakashan, Durga Guri, New Darjeeling More, Siliguri, by Santiraj Sharma.

Globalization and Labour- Management Relations: Dynamics of Change, Response Books, New Delhi, 2001 by C.S. Venkata Ratnam.

Productivity and Labour in Tea Plantations in India, 2008, Siliguri, *Tea Despatch* (a Journal), by Prof. Sharit Bhowmik.

Brief Notes on Gorkhaland, 2009, Gorkha Janakmukti Aadivasi Morcha, Jaigaon, West Bengal, 2009 by Dr. Sonam B. Wangyal.

The Nepalis of North East India, Concept Publishing House, New Delhi, T.B.Subba and A. C. Sinha, 2008.

Ehtnicity, State and Development, Har Anand Publication, New Delhi, 1990, by T. B.Subba.

Essays on Socio- Political Analysis of Sikkimese Society, 2010, Das Printers, Siliguri by T.N. Sharma.

History of All India Gorkha League, 1943-1949, Nirmal Publishers and Distributors, New Delhi, 1987 by B.N. Singh and Kirpal Singh.

Ghuk Dai Na Ghuk Ne Pahar Ko Choro (in Nepali) Pratima Publications, Siliguri, 1997 by Prof. Mohan P. Dahal, University of North Bengal.

Samarao Samidha (in Nepali), Pratima Publication,

Siliguri, 2003 by Prof. Mohan P. Dahal, University of North Bengal.

Challenges of Tea Management in Twenty First Century, N.L. Publishers, Dibrugargh (Assam), 2000 by Dr. S.S. Chaudhury

Employment and Unionization in Indian Industry, Friederich Ebert Stiftung, New Delhi, 1995 by Sarath Davala.

Competitiveness in Global Tea Trade, Oxford University Press, New Delhi, 2004 by V.N. Asopa.

Tea Industry in Transition, Abhijeet Publications, New Delhi, 2009 by Gangadhar Banerjee and Srijeet Banerji.

The Road of Destiny: Darjeeling Letters, 1939, Oxford University Press, 1986 by Fred Pinn.

The Story of Darjeeling, Mani Printing Press, Darjeeling, 2008 and 2009 by Basant B.Lama.

Gorkhaland Movement: A Cladestine Invasion, Janakchetna, Siliguri, 2009 by Dr. D.P.Kar.

Between Sikkim and Bhutan, B.R. Publishing Corporation, Delhi, 1978, Indira Awasty.

Darjeeling: A Favoured Retreat, Indus Publishing Company, New Delhi, 1989, Jahar Sen.

Hamro Basbhumi Chiyabari Mazdoor Anodolanko Pahilo Charan Pheri naya Charan (in Nepali) Computer Centre, Darjeeling, 2000 by R.B. Rai.

Making Globalization Work, Alan Lane, London, 2007 by Joseph E. Stiglitz.

Economic Daualism and Structure of Class, Cosmo Publication, New Delhi, 1997 by Virginius Xaxa.

Class Formation in the Plantation System, People's Publishing House, Delhi, 1981, Sharit Bhowmik.

Concise History of the Darjeeling District since 1835 with a complete Itinerary of Tours in Sikkim and the District, Jetsun Publishing House, Calcutta, Darjeeling, Vanarasi, 1989 by E.C. Dozey.

Rethinking Gorkha Identity, Outside the Imperium of Discourse, Harmony and History, 2010 by Prof. Bidhan Golay on Website, University of North Bengal, Darjeeling, West Bengal.

The Marginalized Gorkhas in West Bengal by Dr. Khemraj Sharma, 2010, pubslihed in *Madhya Marga,* a monthly Nepaliu magazine, Siliguri.

Women Tea Plantation Workers in India, 1991, Heritage Publishers, New Delhi by Dr. Mita Bhadra.

Caste-Tribe Mobility in India and the Case of Kumaon Bhotias by Shri Ram P. Srivastava in Christoph Von Furer Haimendorf(Ed.) *Caste and Kin in Nepal, India and Ceylon: Anthropological Studies in Hindu-Budhist Contact Zone,* Asia Publishing House, Bombay, 1966.

Working Class in India: Hisotry of Emergence and Mcvement (1830-1970), K.P. Bagchi and Company, Ananda Press and Publication, Calcutta, 1977 by Sukomal Sen.

Indo- Nepal Migration, A Seminar paper presented at the University of North Bengal, Centre for Himalayan Studies, Darjeeling, 1985 by Kamsakar.

Basic Problems of Plantation Workers, International Labour Organisation, Geneva, 1950.

Statistical account of Bengal, "Darjeeling", Government Printing Press, Alipore, Calcutta, 1876, by W.W. Hunter.

"Ne-Bu-La: A movement for Regional Solidarity" in K.S. Singh (Ed.) *Tribal Movement in India,* Manohar Publications, New Delhi, 1982, by A.K. Danda and S.B. bagchi.

Industrial Sociology, Educational Publishers, Agra, 1992, by Dr. Kumar.

Darjeeling, Shyam Prakashan, Darjeeling, 1979 by Nar Bahadur Gurung.

Bas Salki Rahecha (in Nepali), 1981, Deepak Press, Benaras, by Bhagirath Rawat.

Mato Ko Maya (in Nepali) Deepak Press, Benaras, 1982 by Bhagirat Rawat.

History of Arunachal Pradesh, Concept Publishing Company, New Delhi, 1997 by M.L. Bose.

"Nepal" in S.K. Chatterjee (Ed.) *Cultural Heritage of India,* Vol.5, Government Printing Press, Alipore, Calcutta, 1978 by Paras Mani Pradhan.

Honey Bee, CBWE Publication, Nagpur, 1986 by G. Ramanujam.

Fatalism and Development: Nepal's Struggle for Modernisation, Orient Longman, Calcutta, 1993 by Dor Bahadur Bista.

A Study of Nepali Economic History (1768-1846), Manjushri Publication, New Delhi, 1971 by Prof. Mahesh Chandra Regmi.

Prisoners of the Past, Is Karat Living in 1940s? An article

by Amulya Ganguli, in *The Statesman* (Newspaper-Daily) from Siliguri published on 1.11.2010.

Plantation Economy in Third World, Vikas Publishing House, New Delhi, 1989 by Uma Devi.

'Strikes more Political than Labour-based" an interview with Shri Harish Rawat, Union Minister for Labour and Employment, Government of India being published in *Statesman* (Daily Newspaper) published from Siliguri on 20.11.2010.

Planter's Raj to Swaraj, ICHR, New Delhi, 1977 by Amalendu Guha.

Labour Under Globalization, 2009, Abhijeet Publications, New Delhi, by K. Chitra.